Why vote Plaid Cymru

Adam Price MP

with a foreword by Ieuan Wyn Jones

First published in Great Britain in 2010 by
Biteback Publishing Ltd
Heal House
375 Kennington Lane
London
SE11 5QY

ISBN 978-1-84954-036-0

10 9 8 7 6 5 4 3 2 1

A CIP catalogue record for this book is available from the British Library.

Set in Garamond
Printed and bound in Great Britain by CPI Cox & Wyman, Reading, RG1 8EX.

Contents

Left to right: Dafydd Elis-Thomas AM, Presiding Officer of the Welsh Assembly; Ieuan Wyn Jones AM, Plaid Cymru Leader; Dafydd Wigley, Plaid Cymru honorary president.

Foreword

At a time when people in Wales have never felt so angry and let down by the same old politics in Westminster, more and more are turning to Plaid because they know that it offers something different.

They know that our party's values are in tune with those of our communities – they are the values of fairness and social justice upon which the politics of modern Wales were built. Which other party in Wales can make that same claim? Think about it.

Labour has slavishly followed Tory policies for twelve years, and Cameron has modelled himself and his politics on Tony Blair. The London-based parties are funded by the same big corporations, banks and millionaires that led the UK into this financial and economic mess. Now, their slash-and-burn policies are threatening to damage our public services irreparably.

Welsh communities deserve better. As we enter a new decade Plaid will demonstrate that it not only understands that feeling of despair and lack of trust in politicians – but that it has become a vehicle to inspire people to renew their faith in politics.

Which party loves Wales's communities and cares about creating a better future for its children? Which party will best stand up for Wales's interests? Who will make the biggest difference? Yet another Labour, Tory or Lib Dem to toe the London party line, or an independent-thinking Plaid MP who always puts their area first?

They are Westminster's voice in Wales.

Plaid will always be Wales's voice in Westminster.

Ieuan Wyn Jones AM, Plaid Cymru Leader

Preface

Why vote Plaid? Answering this question in almost 40,000 words is no mean feat. Most of the time, Plaid Cymru elected members and activists are usually seeking the silver bullet answer to that very question in a five-second time space. After all, that's often in reality how much time they may have on the doorstep. Our political culture is now bitesized. Our news is 24-hour, fast-changing, citizen centred. Mainstream news can often hinge on who said what in what blog, and a catalogue of political events can be catalysed by an imprudent 140-character message on Twitter. The traditional public political meeting has been exchanged for virtual political forums where contributors hide behind a veil of anonymity or a comical *nom de plume*. All of this means that the opportunity to write in depth about Plaid (as is the case for any political party) is now rare and manifestos don't always give the space to write much about the political backdrop to our ideas and policy proposals. So this opportunity in *Why Vote Plaid* to cover our philosophical core, our principles and what the party hopes to achieve in policy terms in both the short term and long term is welcome. The book is aimed at the undecided, floating voter who has no permanent political home, or indeed at anyone who has an interest in politics or Wales. But inevitably, it is intended mainly for those who exercise their right to vote in Wales (although it is hoped that voters reading this elsewhere in the world will find it interesting and relevant).

Plaid: the basics

To begin at the beginning, as Dylan Thomas once said, for anyone who thinks that Plaid is a type of tightly woven thick material made of wool, perhaps it should be explained at the outset that Plaid is shorthand for Plaid Cymru or, to give the party its full legal name, Plaid Cymru The Party of Wales (quite a mouthful!). Most people in Wales refer to Plaid Cymru (which translates from the Welsh language as 'The Party of Wales') as Plaid (pronounced *pla-eed*). In this book both 'Plaid' and 'Plaid Cymru' will be used interchangeably.

Established in 1925, Plaid is broadly defined as a left-leaning nationalist political party. It is a sister party of the SNP and a member of the Greens/European Free Alliance group in the European Parliament. Plaid wasn't always a political party in that its early years are more characteristic of a mass movement or pressure group. More information can be found as to Plaid's political values and principles later on in this book. The quick-fire answer to the question 'What is Plaid?' is that we are a political party that wants independence for Wales in the European Union. That aspiration is a long-term aim, subject to the will of the people of Wales. That is, Plaid believes that independence will only come about when the people of Wales declare their support for it in a referendum. Plaid believes that Wales's people have the right to make decisions for themselves and believes in independence... recognising that this can only be achieved if the people of Wales want it. In the meantime, Plaid is no different to any other political party. It fights elections at all levels of government based on a party manifesto and has elected members at all levels (councillors, AMs, MPs, MEPs) in all parts of Wales. Plaid's logo is that of the Welsh poppy (*Meconopsis cambrica* to give it its Latin name) and not the daffodil as often assumed. It is the only poppy which is indigenous to Europe. It germinates in spring and, in wet and dry conditions alike, puts down deep and lasting roots. In summer, it flowers yellow and is bright like the sun. The Welsh poppy is the inspiration for Plaid's visual identity. The image itself is simple and striking. Like the poppy, Plaid too has strong, sustaining roots. It too has been nurtured – and continues to grow – through winter storms and summer breezes.

Plaid sees its duty as representing Wales and the people of Wales first and last. Plaid wants to make Wales a better place in which to live and work. The people of Wales suffer the highest levels of ill health and are among the poorest in western Europe. Plaid wants a proper Parliament that is capable of releasing the nation's potential and that has the tools to do the job properly. Our short-term political goal is to secure a referendum on law-making powers for Wales in those policy areas which are devolved and for this to be achieved by the next round of Assembly elections in 2011. Put simply, this is because Plaid believes that in order for Wales to become a wealthier, healthier and more prosperous nation, the National Assembly for Wales needs further legislative powers. A proper parliament with law-making powers in devolved fields would be elected by the people of Wales, be run for the benefit of the people of Wales and be answerable to the people of Wales. It would end Westminster's power to veto democratic decisions, which is an insult to the sovereignty of the people of Wales and to the principles of democracy itself.

Why vote at all?

Of course, the greatest challenge in this current climate, where politics and politicians have lost all credibility and respect, is that all political parties must be able to address the question 'Why vote at all?' Restoring trust in the political system is about much more than reforming the expenses system. It's about addressing the root causes of apathy and asking why people have lost faith. It's about putting democracy back at the heart of those traditional institutions – such as Westminster – which have failed the people so spectacularly. While all those who have an interest in democracy must surely be concerned at the damage done to the political system, especially given recent scandals in Westminster, Plaid has always seen the need to reform the corrupt, undemocratic and failing 'Mother of Parliaments'. Of course, Plaid has never been complacent about the need for reform because change is at the core of the party's political philosophy. As a party, we exist to change the nature of UK politics. The need for root and branch reform might not have been obvious to most before now. Yet it has always been one of Plaid's key principles. To Plaid, Westminster has always represented a distant and uncaring political tradition which has seen Wales at the periphery of its affairs and treated it as such. But it now seems that Plaid's position has been more than vindicated.

People from all over the UK are sick of the same old politics from the same old political parties who put self-preservation and the interest of the few (wealthy bankers and big business) ahead of ordinary people. The London-based parties and their broken system have let Wales down. Indeed, they have let everyone down. Government after government has had the opportunity to reform yet those opportunities have been wasted. So, if there's one thing that people know, it's that Plaid has never been in politics in order to preserve the cosy Westminster club. Plaid has campaigned for decades to democratise the unfit, unjust House of Lords, for instance, to end its patronage, to introduce proportional representation and to make Westminster more representative of the people and communities it exists to serve. The advent of devolution a decade ago, with new institutions in Wales, Scotland and Northern Ireland and their transparent, open and plural political cultures, inevitably meant that, sooner or later, Westminster's failings would come to light. The anachronistic, out-of-touch, deferential traditions of old certainly have compared unfavourably with the new political norm in the Senedd, Holyrood and Stormont.

Restoring trust in politics

It seems that in this political climate, everyone sees the need to restore trust in politics. The very essence of our democracy is under threat. Plaid Cymru elected members are different from the others in that they are not, and will never want to be, part of the corrupt Westminster system. Plaid elected members are ordinary people who do not belong to the money-fuelled, privileged London clique. Plaid is a people-centric, people-focused party – the true party of the people in communities all over Wales. The need for reform isn't just about expenses either. The political class is damaged as a result of the expenses scandal but that comes hot on the heels of the banking crisis in the middle of a ravaging recession. So at a time when people are suffering as a result of the credit crunch, when people are worried about paying the bills and the sense of insecurity that this brings, there is an ever greater sense of injustice when bank executives are seen to be on the take and when politicians are perceived to be fleecing a corrupt system to inflate their already generous salaries. Those privileges, which elites might have taken for granted at one point and which the public would once have put up with, are no longer tolerated. Deference for politicians is no more. These changes happening to society are, it could be argued, indicative of a more fundamental change. There is a shift away from all things big – big business, big banks, big bonuses (which are all examples of authority) – with the focus shifting to the personal, the local and the familiar. People want to place their trust in someone or something that they know and value. There is evidence of this with Obama's election. The decentralised, people-empowered and grassroots nature of his campaign was all about people coming together for a greater good ('Yes we can') along with the circumnavigating of traditional power structures. Likewise, the explosion in citizen journalism, blogging, Twitter and social networking sites suggests the same. Each and every voice has a value in its own right (and individuals feel empowered to have a voice in the first place). This is symptomatic of a movement away from traditional power structures and the democratisation of politics itself. Plaid understands this shift because as a party, it has been on the margins of these structures and has long championed the need for change.

So enough is enough! No more of the same. Plaid understands that people are angry and want change. Plaid understands the day-to-day difficulties that people face. Plaid MPs **are** independent minded – they're willing to fight for their constituents and are not swayed by the interests of London bosses because there are no London bosses to please.

What's the role of a Plaid MP?

So why send elected members to Westminster at all? What is the role of a Plaid MP? Is it hypocritical to criticise Westminster yet to go there to do a job of work? Plaid's position is clear. For as long as decisions affecting the lives of people in Wales are made in London, Plaid has a duty to ensure that it plays its part in serving and protecting the interests of the people of Wales in Parliament. This has always been the way. Our first ever MP, Gwynfor Evans, elected in a dramatic by-election in 1966, was often referred to as 'the member for Wales'. After all, Plaid MPs' only loyalties are to their constituents, their community and their nation. Plaid can never be part of the Westminster establishment. We may again hold the balance of power (as we did in the 1970s with Callaghan in government). We may be the kingmakers in a likely hung Parliament, but we will never forget that Westminster is our means to an end and not the end in itself. So what is 'the end', particularly as we look forward to the next set of Westminster elections in 2010?

Plaid's primary locus of power, in order to initiate change on behalf of the people of Wales, is the National Assembly for Wales. This youngest of democracies is the vehicle by which we want to change our nation for the better and our goal is to lead our nation in government. For now, Plaid is part of the One Wales coalition government with Labour in the National Assembly for Wales (forged following the 2007 National Assembly elections). Coalitions are an inevitable consequence of a political system which uses proportional representation. It's an honour for Plaid, after eighty-four years in opposition, to be able to start to deliver on its policies and priorities. In order to achieve our programme of change in government, and for as long as our decision-making processes involve the to-ing and fro-ing of legislative measures back and forth between the Senedd in Cardiff Bay and Whitehall, Plaid MPs have a vital role to play.

- Plaid MPs are needed in Westminster to help deliver the One Wales government's legislative programme in the face of the undemocratic, disgraceful Westminster veto which could be exercised at the whim of the secretary of state.

- In the possible scenario of a hung Parliament, where no one party has outright control after the 2010 Westminster elections, a Celtic Alliance of Plaid and SNP MPs could hold the balance of power securing major concessions for Wales and Scotland.

- Voters in Wales must remember the mantra 'No change Brown'. Gordon Brown doesn't offer anything new – he's a joint co-author and co-architect, along with Blair, of the New Labour project. His politics in fact represent 'more of the same' and Plaid MPs must expose his New Labour credentials.

- The Tories and Labour represent two sides of the same coin – they both represent the London consensus, which has failed and is continuing to fail Wales.
- Plaid is delivering in government for the people of Wales and has led a number of changes from saving hospital services in Wales to introducing measures to curb bovine TB to dealing with the ravages of the recession.

While this tells you what Plaid MPs are about and what they see as their main priorities, it doesn't tell you much about our fundamental beliefs. So, what is Plaid about?

What's Plaid about?

For many who are unfamiliar with Plaid or are new to Welsh politics, Plaid is often seen as a single-issue party. Plaid is also sometimes perceived to be a party exclusively for Welsh speakers or is seen as a party that wants to separate Wales from the rest of the world. Of course, Plaid is proud of Wales's unique linguistic heritage and our *raison d'être* hinges on ensuring that Wales's status as a nation in its own right is reflected in the way that it runs its affairs, as self-government is a means to building a different Wales. Plaid doesn't want to separate Wales from the rest of the world. Rather, Plaid wants the nation to take its rightful place as an equal partner, recognised as a nation in its own right as part of the global family. To paraphrase the first ever woman SNP MP, Winnie Ewing, Plaid wants Wales to 'join the world'. Plaid believes that Wales needs a proper parliament to do the job of governing our country properly. So what kind of job would it want that parliament to do? That is, what are its political priorities?

Plaid is a political party with ideas, policies and principled positions on the hundreds of issues and problems which worry voters from Holyhead to Holywell, from Bangor to Bargoed. Plaid's radical edge comes from its roots as a national movement and pressure group and still today, it takes the best from that tradition of political campaigning, fusing it with democratic policy-led political action.

So what does Plaid Cymru stand for? What are our aims? What do we believe in? What do we represent? Who are Plaid people? Why do people join and support Plaid? What is their motivation?

Plaid is a party of ordinary people from all over Wales and is not a party of one corner of Wales, neither Cardiff Bay nor the *crachach* (a pejorative term for the elite). Plaid is a party of people who care passionately about Wales's land, its people and its future. That's the very nature of Plaid's nationalism, a positive love of Wales and its people. Plaid wants the nation, its young people and its young democracy to have every chance to succeed. Our politics is not the politics of envy or blame, it is the politics of democratic aspiration – for a better quality of life for everyone. That sense of aspiration and success means that we need people in Parliament who will stand up, speak up and always put Wales first. That's the core of our political message: our only loyalty is to Wales and its people. Of course, that statement tells you everything and nothing. It tells you about our basic, most fundamental motivation but it doesn't tell you much about the type of Wales and the kind of world in which we want to live.

The type of Wales that we want to create is one typified by *chwarae teg*, or fairness. Fairness is primarily about ensuring that everyone has access to economic democracy and social justice. Fundamental to our politics in Plaid is a belief that economic inequality lies at the heart of many, if not most, of our social problems and ills. The root causes of crime, poor health and low educational attainment could all be tackled if we were equal economically.

So, in order for us to live in a fairer society, Plaid believes:

- Everyone who works should earn a liveable wage and should be able to send their children to university.

- People who earn the most should pay the most for the benefit they receive from living here.
- People should look after the environment so as not to harm the living or compromise the safety of future generations.
- The elimination of poverty, at home and abroad, is one of our most important responsibilities.
- Wales's culture and language are a precious inheritance that we must protect and preserve for future generations.
- Tolerance and mutual respect are the hallmarks of a civilised society.

These principles of fairness are at the foundation of our policies. Those policies are created by our members. Plaid is led by its members from the grassroots. Our members create our policies in our annual conference and they hold the party's elected leadership to account. Plaid has at least two conferences every year, and often holds one-day conferences on specific issues as well. While democratic politics in the UK has been marred by the way in which the three London-based parties do not listen to their members and have found ways and means of sidelining the ordinary people within their ranks, Plaid is different in that its members are the bedrock of the organisation.

Plaid is different

As a member-led organisation, Plaid retains its radical edge. Indeed, for those who don't believe in politics as usual, Plaid is their party. Since Plaid was established, it's always believed in Wales. Plaid doesn't just act differently to the other London-based parties, it is fundamentally different. After all, there are no London party lines to toe. Plaid members decide on the party's ideas, policies and action plans. There is no such thing as a Plaid elite. Plaid believes that every single member and supporter has something to contribute, whether that's delivering newsletters to neighbours, organising a fund-raising event, becoming a blogger or making sandwiches at election time for other party workers. Everyone can play his or her part in creating a better Wales. As for the party's staff, they're based all over Wales (in one of twenty offices for both the party and its elected members) and at our headquarters (Tŷ Gwynfor, named after Plaid's first MP, Gwynfor Evans) in Cardiff. People can keep up to date with what Plaid representatives and staff are doing by going to www.plaidcymru.org or www.plaidlive.com or by reading our party newspapers (*Y Ddraig Goch* and *Welsh Nation*), which are published at least once a quarter. Plaid depends solely on members and supporters' contributions for funding so doesn't have to pander to the whims of any business or individual. Of course Plaid listens and speaks to charities, companies and campaigning organisations who, like us, want to create a better Wales . . . but you won't find Plaid politicians courting oligarchs on any yachts in the Med any time soon!

Apparently, people aren't joining political parties any more but being a member of Plaid is enjoyable and rewarding so it's important that Plaid events are fun and buzzing. That's why our conferences are brimming with things to do (from debates and discussion to music, comedy and good food!). We want people to actually have a good time being a Plaid member . . . so we don't want things to be boring!

Plaid is led by Assembly Member Ieuan Wyn Jones (who represents the Ynys Môn constituency at the National Assembly for Wales). He holds the Economic Development and Transport portfolio and is currently Deputy First Minister of Wales since Plaid entered the One Wales coalition government following the 2007 elections to the National Assembly. Plaid has the second highest number of Assembly Members in Wales (second to Labour) and has three ministers and one deputy minister in the Cabinet. At a local level, Plaid again has the second highest number of county councillors belonging to a political party, with 210. Since the 2008 local elections, Plaid has shared control in nine out of Wales's twenty-two local authorities, including Cardiff, Wales's capital city. At a European level, Plaid has one MEP (out of Wales's four), while in Westminster we currently have three MPs out of Wales's forty.

How we campaign

Plaid recognises that we cannot compete with the three mainstream, London-based parties in the UK-wide media – the vast majority of people in Wales still get the bulk of their news from UK network TV and the London-based papers. However, a very considerable and rapidly increasing proportion of the population are receiving news online. Plaid emulates the techniques of some of the US election campaigns to level this playing field. Some political strategists are already looking at using the web to develop their future support – a 'fifty-year strategy' looking at bringing younger people into the party early through the web. Considering the vast potential vote from the 'Welsh-identifying' younger generations in Wales, this has added importance for a movement like Plaid. Plaid has already gained a reputation as a pioneering, innovative and technologically driven party by dramatically developing our use of the internet and new media. This will be developed to communicate with our own members, potential voters, and to influence journalist and the media.

Change in mindset

Plaid is moving away from the mindset of having a static website and little else. Internet campaigning is no different from 'normal' campaigning. It has become 'normalised' as part of Plaid's campaigning rather than thought of as 'ad hoc', and Plaid is seen as being in the vanguard of e-campaigning among political parties in Wales and further afield. Human and financial resources have been allocated to ensure that our web presence is effective. The term 'web presence' is used because people traditionally have though it sufficient to have a standard website and little else. The growth of social networking and what is known as Web 2.0 means that Plaid must look at all aspects of the web to ensure our goals are being achieved, and this explains the explosion of Plaid activity on line through aggregated websites such as plaidlive.com, the well-known social networking sites and Plaid-owned campaigning websites such as walescan.com.

Plaid principles

While the other parties organise themselves across the UK, Plaid Cymru only fields candidates in Wales. Basic demographics mean that Wales will be sidelined as far as the other parties' priorities are concerned. Labour, Tories and Lib Dems – the London-based parties – are ultimately all the same. Their politics are so similar in content and tone that it's difficult to distinguish between them nowadays. That hasn't always been the case, of course, but Labour has abandoned its supporters, its original values and ethos by slavishly following Tory policies for twelve years. Cameron likewise has modelled himself on Tony Blair. In this topsy-turvy world, all three parties at Westminster agree on everything from tax to war to 'the special relationship' with the US.

The London parties are funded by the same big corporations, banks and millionaires that have created the economic mess which is impacting the poorest most. For Plaid, elections shouldn't be about the big London parties and their usual narratives and policies based on attracting the support of those in the south-east of England. For Plaid, elections should be about the people and communities of Wales. After all, while most families in Wales are struggling to tread water, Labour and Tory politicians are on the same millionaire's yacht in the Mediterranean taking the same big donations from oligarchic millionaires. The London political class live on a different planet when compared to most people in Wales, and debates on landmark issues such as inheritance tax (with neither Tory nor Labour proposals doing anything to help the average family in Wales) simply underline this divide.

The other London-based parties are Westminster's voice in Wales. Plaid is Wales's voice in Westminster. London-party MPs do what they're told. They say they represent Wales in Westminster, but we know that they represent Westminster's rule over Wales. The way that the majority of Welsh MPs from the other parties vote on key issues, be they the future of the Post Office network, reforming the banks or the war in Afghanistan (which are at odds with the views of the majority of people in Wales), shows this. If people want a truly independent voice to deliver for their community, only Plaid can offer it. Because who's really going to stand up for our communities? Is it the representatives of that cosy Westminster club or Plaid MPs, whose only loyalty is to the people of Wales? After all, a Labour MP recently said that elections are won and lost in the south-east of England. That's how much a Welsh Labour or Tory vote counts: not a jot. Another Tory or Labour MP in Westminster won't make a difference for Wales but a Plaid MP will. Plaid MPs have always had a reputation for punching above their weight and getting the best for their area. Plaid MPs will never be there just to make up the numbers like so many of the London party MPs.

Is Plaid anti-English?

While Plaid has always seen its focus as being the National Assembly for Wales and recognises the inherent asymmetry of the British state, Plaid seeks a relationship of equality for Wales and England. Some of course want to reap political capital by accusing Plaid of being anti-English. But Plaid only wants for Wales what England has and also supports the campaign for an English Parliament. It should come as no surprise that many English incomers to Wales support Plaid because they too recognise that Wales is losing out on the periphery of the UK. They recognise that in order to thrive, Wales needs the ability to develop that all-important sense of self-confidence and self-belief that is critical to a nation's success.

So, the time of Wales being held back by its lack of self-belief is ending. Wales is growing in confidence with every generation. This is not the time for the Wales Cannot generation. Rather, it's the time for the WalesCan generation – the independence generation where, thanks to devolution, more and more people believe that decisions about Wales should be made in Wales. This has nothing to do with being anti-English but rather about recognising the sovereignty of the people of Wales along with the unequal nature of the British state. So, why do some peddle the myth that being pro-Welsh independence means you're anti-English?

Thinking back to the 2007 Assembly elections in Wales, what would someone have learned about them had you been dependent on the output of the London press and broadcast media? Next to nothing. The 'forgotten contest' (as *The Guardian* described it, while simultaneously failing to do anything very much to un-forget it) took very much a back seat to the same day's polls for the Scottish Parliament and the English town halls. The Scottish election in particular was followed rigorously from London, but for one reason alone. The SNP were considerably ahead in the polls and managed (just) to maintain that lead into forming a minority government at Holyrood. To the British (or rather, the London) media, this build-up was war. They hit the nuclear button, and filled their pages and airtime with often-hysterical doom-mongering about how this would break up Britain, shatter consensus and pitch Scots against English in a way not seen since Bannockburn. It is striking that there wasn't one positive statement about how the situation could be anything other than a disaster in the making.

Of course, Plaid believes that it is perfectly possible to feel passionately fond of all the countries and cultures of the islands of Britain. This is *always* the starting point for the debate as to what kind of political settlement the countries of the UK should be seeking in the twenty-first century. To be for Welsh or Scottish independence is automatically inferred to be stridently, even violently, anti-English. You love one so much, you have viscerally to hate the other. The debate is only ever presented in such stark, oppositional terms, and it does it a huge disservice. It is perfectly possible to feel passionately fond of all the countries and cultures of our islands. Plaid wants to see them all thrive, without having to believe that the anachronism of the UK is the only way to achieve that.

Because for Plaid, it is an anachronism. The United Kingdom of Great Britain and Ireland was explicitly created in 1801 as a product of, and engine for, the industrial, military and colonial age, functions it has unswervingly fulfilled ever since. Two centuries on, society should have the courage to recognise that that era has drawn to a close and seek to work out the best blueprint for its collective future. And each of the (in this instance) three (England, Wales and Scotland) is a natural nation, one that has been consistently defined – geographically and culturally – for more than 1,500 years.

Plaid politics

While so far this book has focused on some of the political, historical and social context for Plaid's ideas, this section focuses on some of our broad-brush principles. After all, all political parties have a set of values or principles which are the driving force behind their ideas, policies and priorities for government. Plaid's political DNA can be broadly defined as left of centre, decentralist socialist, green, nationalist and internationalist with a healthy dose of scepticism about free markets and globalisation (in the economic sense).

Plaid's constitution defines its aims as follows:

- to promote the constitutional advancement of Wales with a view to attaining full national status for Wales within the European Union;
- to ensure economic prosperity, social justice and the health of the natural environment, based on decentralist socialism;
- to build a national community based on equal citizenship, respect for different traditions and cultures and the equal worth of all individuals, whatever their race, nationality, gender, colour, creed, sexuality, age, ability or social background;
- to create a bilingual society by promoting the revival of the Welsh language;
- to promote Wales's contribution to the global community and to attain membership of the United Nations.

These aims underpin our politics. So where do they come from? As we look forward to our eighty-fifth birthday as a party, Plaid's development isn't easily divorced from the history of Wales (with key landmarks such as the drowning of Capel Celyn, the establishment of S4C, the 1979 and 1997 referenda) or from events the world over (such as the fight against apartheid and nuclear arms), as Plaid is a party which follows the maxim 'Think globally, act locally'. The party's unequivocal opposition to both the Iraq war and the war in Afghanistan (let alone the alleged 'war on terror') is one indication of our international outlook. So too is our record on promoting peace in the Middle East and in other areas of conflict and on promoting human rights and civil liberties. Perhaps it's more important for a nationalist party like Plaid to show that its nationalism is not fuelled by bigotry, hatred and xenophobia but rather by a deep-seated love for our nation and a commitment to serve all those who have chosen to make Wales their home regardless of their background. So where are Plaid Cymru's historical roots? How did it develop into the political party that it has become today?

Plaid Cymru's roots

The anachronistic nature of the British state is one of the reasons given as to why the founding members of Plaid Cymru came together in the early 1920s. But what were the other reasons for establishing the party? Key among them was a sense of injustice facing the people of Wales, which compelled the founding members to form a political party in 1925. Other quasi-political organisations (such as Cymru Fydd and the Welsh Movement) had been in existence but there was no single political expression for the wish to establish a government in Wales. While each founding member of Plaid had different political motivations for wanting to establish the party, the unifying thread was a deep-seated anxiety for the future of Wales's people and their communities. After all, the First World War was fresh in the memories of some of those early members who had fought so that other small nations across Europe could be free. This personal experience of seeing other small nations gain independence only served to underline the sense of indifference and injustice which faced Wales in socio-economic, cultural and political terms.

Lewis Valentine, Saunders Lewis and Gwynfor Evans are prominent figures in the development of Plaid Cymru. Valentine was the party's first president. Lewis, an academic and dramatist, was party president between 1926 and 1939. Evans, the party's first Member of Parliament, was president between 1945 and 1981, when Dafydd Wigley (the party's current honorary president) took over.

Other figures that have contributed to the party's political appeal include the author Kate Roberts, who helped shape the party's socialist policies. D. J. and Noelle Davies built on their knowledge of Irish and Scandinavian economic policy and wrote the seminal text *Can Wales Afford Self-Government?*, the answer to which was a resounding 'Yes!'. The Cambridge academic Raymond Williams came to prominence as a Plaid Cymru member in the 1970s. These diverse key figures have all contributed to Plaid Cymru's achievements in all corners of Wales and have left a historical legacy which is rich in its variety and which have led some to describe Plaid as a broad church.

Four years into its existence, Plaid contested its first parliamentary election in Caernarfon at the UK general election of May 1929. Valentine was the party's candidate, and he polled 609 votes. These 609 electors became known as 'the gallant six hundred' when Dafydd Iwan, current party president, immortalised them in song. Just over forty years later, Plaid Cymru was to take and hold this seat with a convincing majority. After World War II, the presidency of the late Gwynfor Evans proved a catalyst to the party's growth and development. In the UK General Election of 1950, Plaid Cymru fielded seven candidates. By 1964 this number had grown to twenty-three. Membership of the party grew rapidly during the late 1960s and constituency organisations were formed in many new areas. Following Gwynfor Evans's sensational victory in the 1966 Carmarthen Westminster by-election, Plaid also came within a whisker of breaking the Labour stranglehold (Wales's traditional hegemony) in two key valley by-elections at Rhondda West in 1967 and Caerffili in 1968. In 1970, the party contested all seats in Wales for the first time in its history and polled over 175,000 votes. Today, of course, Plaid contests every seat for the European Parliament, Westminster and the National Assembly along with a great number of local council seats in all councils.

Plaid women

As Laura McAllister, author of the first full-length study of Plaid Cymru noted, 'the role of women in the political history of Wales is a hugely unexplored area.' This may be expected considering that since 1918 only seven women have represented Wales as MPs. Until 1997, there had only been four women MPs in Wales's political history. There has never been a woman Plaid Cymru MP, and the party is still waiting for its first female Plaid Cymru president. But this is not a true reflection of the party's history, or of the political process in Wales. Looking back we can clearly see that women have been very involved in our political history. Be it the suffragette movement, the campaigns for a parliament for Wales, the activities of the Welsh-language pressure group Cymdeithas yr Iaith, the efforts of women during the miners' strike, the protest at Greenham Common, or more recently against the war in Iraq. All are examples of women reacting to their political environment. Women have always played an influential, controversial and intellectual role in the development of Plaid.

Indeed, it's thanks to a woman that Plaid exists at all. In 1924 a number of young Welsh men felt the desire to place their nationalism at the heart of their politics. There were two movements, one in South Wales led by Saunders Lewis and Ambrose Bebb, and another in North Wales led and organised by H. R. Jones. Mai Roberts, private secretary to the Liberal MP E. T. John, was integral to the union of both movements that formed Plaid Cymru. She aided and persuaded then General Secretary (of Plaid Cymru) H.R. Jones to contact Saunders Lewis, and should have been present with the six at the famous founding meeting at Pwllheli, North Wales in 1925. Unfortunately she arrived just as the meeting was closing. In 1926 she was invited to be a member of the first formal National Executive.

And just as a woman was influential at the point of its inception, Plaid has equally encouraged women to play an active role throughout the development of the party. In March 1928, an advertisement under the title 'Women in Public Life' was published in *Y Ddraig Goch* (the party newspaper). It stated, 'The National Party believes in giving women a full chance to play their part in politics and public life.' This was a strong commitment in a conservative time, prompted perhaps by the fact that key women during this period were contributing in various fields. This is a clear sign that Plaid Cymru's commitment to equality has been integral from the founding of the party. From administrating to raising money, from standing as candidates to developing policy, from the early formative years to the present day, women have played an influential role in the shaping of the party, and one such key individual is the canonical Welsh author Kate Roberts. Kate Roberts was unsure about joining the party at the beginning and commented, 'I really cannot see myself any nearer to joining the Blaid [sic; 'Plaid' mutated to 'Blaid'] after reading the *Ddraig Goch*. I can see Mr Saunders Lewis's point of view as I love literature, but as I am a Socialist. I really cannot reconcile myself with his ideas.'

However, she did join, became a member of the first formal national executive, and was elected as the first chair of the Women's Section. She went on to become a prominent member, and was very active in the Tonypandy branch all through the 1930s. She wrote articles for the *Ddraig Goch* calling on women to educate themselves politically, to read the manifesto thoroughly, and to speak clearly and concisely when campaigning. She promoted socialism, travelled all over Wales speaking at meetings as a representative of the party and organised great bazaars to collect money.

Noelle Davies, another prominent member, co-wrote many of the party's economic policies alongside her husband D. J. Davies. She is considered a leading force in injecting economic realism into some of the party's policies and was another avid socialist. During the formative years of the party Lady Mallt Williams, who was involved in a number of patriotic movements, contributed vast amounts of money. She contributed the equivalent of £4,000 annually to the party. She helped raise special funds, bought up to 400 copies of Plaid Cymru newspapers to distribute herself each month and secured a financial basis for the party through donations and financial advice. Indeed, in 1927 Saunders Lewis claimed that a contribution of £100 from Lady Mallt had 'saved their lives.'

Mai Roberts, Kate Roberts, Noelle Davies and Lady Mallt Williams's contributions were without doubt diverse, individually unique and different from the contribution of the majority of women in the party in these formative years. Considering that these contributions were made during a period when women often had to choose between marriage and education, the vast contributions and efforts of these women are even more striking. Without doubt, these individuals should be considered role models; perhaps even more so than their male counterparts given the social barriers that they faced. The more common activities of married female members of the time often involved essential fundraising activities such as organising coffee mornings and bazaars. Women also played a key role in the distribution of Plaid Cymru newspapers. During the 1930s they were often seen selling newspapers across Wales. One example mentioned by Kate Roberts is of a 'gentleman' who was approached by a woman in Cardiff and replied, 'no, I don't want it they sell it up in the Rhondda, they are like b****** flies all over the place!' These activities, although not as high profile as certain well-known historical figures and incidents in the party's history, should nevertheless not be overlooked, as they were core to the existence and survival of Plaid Cymru. They were also vital to ensuring the party was accessible to the public, and in particular to other women.

The shocking reality, however, is that until 1999, and the dawn of devolution, Plaid Cymru had no female national elected politicians. Women had been influential and inspiring in elections across the century. Cathrin Huws, who stood for a seat on Cardiff

Council in 1934 at the age of twenty-three, is one such woman. Dr Gwennan Jones, the first woman Westminster candidate, who stood in 1945, is another, as is the dedicated Eileen Beasley, who was not only elected as the first Plaid woman community councillor but had enough strength of character to refuse payment of tax based on the principle that the forms were not available in Welsh, despite regular visits from the bailiffs to her family home. This brave action drew admiration far and wide from leading figures and ordinary people alike. We cannot forget either Jennie Eirian Davies, who stood as a Westminster candidate for Carmarthen in the 1955 and the 1957 by-elections securing 11.5 per cent of the vote, and securing a strong foundation for Gwynfor Evans's historic victory less than ten years later. Jennie Eirian was an inspiration to the women of Plaid Cymru but also to the women of Wales as a woman who decided to do things differently. Former Assembly Member and leader of previously Plaid-controlled Rhondda Cynon Taf Council, Pauline Jarman, is a more recent example of a woman who stands up for her community and her country through her hard work and dedication over the years. She is widely recognised and admired by many.

1979. A historic year for Wales, with a great majority voting against devolution. In the face of such open opposition, Plaid Cymru tried to re-create and re-define itself as a political party. Decentralist socialism became the official core principle and the changing face of society saw a renewed commitment towards the rights of women. In 1981, within a general motion on women's rights, a national conference agreed that 'Plaid Cymru will put its own house in order by giving positive recognition to equal rights through the party structure.'

Consequently, women such as Jill Evans, Helen Mary Jones, Jocelyn Davies and Janet Davies gained prominence and experience, and became some of the party's leading elected members. Today we can consider the nearly equal balance of men and women in our Plaid Cymru Assembly group over the last ten years – a significant step forward. Women have made a massive contribution, in different fields and through different ways. They have defied society and opened our eyes to the fact that we no longer have to choose between family and beliefs. They did, as Plaid does, believe that we can create a better Wales, and their contribution should be celebrated and honoured. At face value, yes, it is easy to draw conclusions that women in the party were not as active as their male counterparts, but in Kate Roberts's own words, writing in the *Ddraig Goch* in January 1950: 'Maybe Plaid women aren't in the limelight, speaking in public and such things, but it's easy and popular to speak on a platform and receive public applause. It's not easy to knock on a door and ask for a vote and receive a derogatory slam of a door in your face.'

History shows only the public face of the party and that is only one element of Plaid Cymru. We must remember that the heart and soul, that has shaped and kept the party going lies in the activities of every member, especially those that have been overlooked by history.

Community socialism

After the shockwaves of 1979 and the party's need to re-discover itself, the party's conference in 1981 incorporated community – or decentralist – socialism into its formal aims and elected Caernarfon MP, Dafydd Wigley as President in succession to Gwynfor Evans. In the same year, Gwynfor (as he's commonly referred to both within and outside Plaid – an indication of his iconic status) took centre stage in the fight for the first Welsh-language television channel, S4C. After a strenuous campaign in which Gwynfor threatened to fast to death, the party forced the Thatcher government into a major concession and secured a Welsh-medium television channel.

In the 1987 election, Ieuan Wyn Jones (now party leader) captured Ynys Môn from the Conservatives.

During the 1990s, Plaid Cymru played a leading role in resisting the Poll Tax and successfully opposed the construction of a giant military radar base at St David's in west Wales. The party also stepped up its bid to secure self-government for Wales in the European Union. The General Election on 9th April 1992 saw Cynog Dafis, on the only ever successful Plaid-Green Party ticket, gaining Ceredigion and Pembroke North from the Liberal Democrats. The party had four MPs.

Plaid recognises the need to ensure that elected politicians represent Wales's communities in all their diversity. Measures to promote women candidates were adopted in the 1990s, which led to the election of six Plaid women to the National Assembly for Wales in 1999. As the new Wales becomes increasingly diverse and multicultural, the party is attracting more members from Wales's ethnic minority communities. The party is proud to have elected the first and only Assembly Member from a BME community. The launch of our youth and student movement, CymruX (see www.cymrux.org) has also drawn a strong cohort of young people to the party with increasing numbers standing in elections on behalf of Plaid Cymru.

Plaid policy positions

The political DNA referred to above is the thread which binds our ideas and policies together. Readers of this booklet will want to know where Plaid stands on bread and butter issues from the economy to the environment to the war in Afghanistan. As is inevitable, there is a great deal of over-lap between these policy areas for which we make no apology recognising the intrinsically holistic and integrated nature of the challenges which we face as a society. This section provides the reader with a synopsis of our policies on the problems and challenges facing both Wales and the wider world. As a party of government in Wales, this section on policy also highlights our work within the One Wales Welsh Assembly government and what further action we believe could be undertaken in Wales to aid the social, environmental and economic recovery of our communities.

Recovering, reforming and renewing the economy

For Plaid, the world economic crisis that began in 2008 may prove to be one of the most significant events in world history in the last hundred years after the two world wars, the birth and death of the Soviet Union, the 'War on Terror' and perhaps its closest comparator, the Great Depression. It is also the case that the economic crisis cannot be divorced from other policy areas such as the environment, transport, housing, taxation policy and community life. The approach to economic recovery must be integrated so this section inevitably touches on a number of policy areas.

It is not an exaggeration to say that it really is only strong political leadership that can help us now. Plaid ministers within the One Wales Welsh Assembly government are doing what they can with the limited powers that are at their disposal, acting swiftly and decisively to protect the skill base of Welsh workers, to support businesses and to help those facing the threat of redundancy or losing their home.

It remains the case, however, that the monopoly over macroeconomic policy, the labour market and trade and financial regulation continues to lie with the UK government in Westminster. It too has a responsibility to the people of Wales. In the midst of one of the worst recessions seen for generations, Plaid believes that a number of measures are necessary for radically overhauling international financial systems, dealing with the consequences of this crisis and developing a more sustainable, greener economy in its aftermath taking into account the impact of the climate crisis on the way we live our lives.

Economic reform, in the short and longer term, at Welsh, UK and European levels, must mean that we map the way from recession towards a new, stronger, more sustainable Welsh economy.

The global financial crisis is hurting all parts of Wales. We in Plaid Cymru recognise and understand the pain caused by growing unemployment, unstable fuel costs and the increasing uncertainty about the future. The current economic crisis is a direct result of the collapse of global financial systems and the failure of regulatory regimes and governments to appreciate not only how it occurred but also its speed and scale.

This crisis was borne of a model of globalisation which gave too much power to corporations and too little protection to workers and consumers. A weak regulatory framework within the banking system – on both sides of the Atlantic – was also undoubtedly a significant part of the problem. Other factors include the rise in private household debt over recent years. Without doubt, the crisis has been exacerbated by this explosion in private household debt, which has grown from 65 per cent of GDP to over 100 per cent in the UK and US. The collapse of both the sub-prime markets in the USA and of Northern Rock in the UK showed the interdependent, complex and interwoven nature of modern global financial systems and how lax regulatory regimes ended up fuelling lending on a scale which was clearly unsustainable. As a result, families have been left saddled with a level of debt they cannot afford to repay and the banks are carrying a level of debt they cannot sustain. The taxpayer is now faced with footing the bill to deal with these so-called 'toxic assets' and yet the bankers still demand their bonuses!

This is also having a detrimental impact on companies. Many are finding that banks are calling in overdrafts and loans are either not available or are very expensive. Successful businesses are being told that the arrangement fee to roll over a loan will be ten times more than the previous fee and companies are cutting back and losing confidence as a result. Furthermore, individual businesses are being forced to reduce costs by making staff redundant, adding a further twist to the downward spiral affecting families and communities across Wales.

The crisis may be global in nature but the UK government has made a number of serious mistakes in its handling of the situation so far. It has failed to understand its gravity, its cause or how it has developed. As a consequence, the UK government's reactions, and those of the Bank of England, have consistently been a case of 'too little, too late'.

Plaid has been familiar with the excesses of the City of London for many years. It has been no secret that successive governments in London have often backed the interests of the City – and indeed the South East of England – at the expense of the rest of the UK. It has certainly been at Wales's expense. It has also been to the detriment of sectors such as manufacturing and this in turn has caused serious economic and social damage to many Welsh communities. It should be remembered that the financial services sector represents a far higher proportion of the economy of the UK – over 8 per cent of GDP – compared with the US or any other major economy. This over-reliance on the financial services sector has been a dangerous imbalance which Plaid Cymru has highlighted over the years.

The UK government's stimulus package has been too timid and unfocused so far to have the desired effect. The action taken to date has largely amounted to a giant insurance policy for the City – a huge safety net for the people who need it least, subsidised by the people who need it most. UK government ministers have also pursued a strategy of announcing initiative after initiative with little coherence, structure or impact and even less focus on outcomes.

Businesses are generally confused as to what help is available, and despite re-capitalisation on a massive scale and government loan guarantees, banks are still very reluctant to lend even to viable and inherently profitable companies. The UK government has allowed this to continue unchallenged. Meanwhile the Conservatives' opposition to any form of fiscal stimulus flies in the face of economic logic at a time when business investment has collapsed and consumer confidence is at rock bottom.

Plaid Cymru's call for a fiscal stimulus as early as November 2008 has been more than vindicated. We wanted to see the tax threshold raised by £2,000 which would have put £400 in the pockets of most taxpayers and taken many low-paid workers out of the tax net altogether. We were also right in condemning the government's cut of 2.5 per cent in VAT as ineffectual, and this proved to be the case with evidence mounting that it has had minimal effect.

In Wales, during the early weeks and months of the recession, jobs were lost at a rate faster than almost any other part of the UK. This was due to the impact on sectors such as construction, automotive and retail. Since then, jobs have not been lost here at the same rate, and the current unemployment level is average for the other nations and regions of the UK.

Nevertheless, the big challenge for Wales as we work our way through this recession is to make the economy sustainable going forward. Economic confidence cannot be restored from the top; we have to water the roots. As things stand, we are too dependent on five to ten year investment decisions by global companies for which we have to compete with many other parts of the world and for which we don't necessarily always represent the best deal by comparison. By moving up the value chain, increasing our share of Research & Development investment and investing in skills at all levels, we can make our economy more resilient and sustainable against cyclical shocks.

Within the Welsh Assembly government, Plaid Cymru, as its record shows, is committed to doing everything in its power to act responsively, swiftly and decisively in the interests of individuals, families and businesses so that Wales is in the best possible position to benefit from the economic upturn when it comes.

We are using all the powers devolved to us in Wales to try and soften the blow of this economic crisis on Welsh communities. As we concentrate on investing in the people of Wales, the UK government bails out the banks with billions and is afraid of upsetting the very bankers who've created this mess.

Indeed, Plaid is dismantling the tribalisms of old in Wales by bringing together ministers, trades unionists, the business community and representatives from the public sector in a series of Economic Summits. These meetings have achieved significant change over a short space of time. Achievements include:

1. Improvements to procurement processes for small and medium enterprises, including faster payments with the Welsh Assembly government now paying 92.5 per cent of invoices within a ten-day target – a vast improvement on previous years.

2. The release of Welsh Assembly government land for new, affordable housing and securing an extra £42 million to help towards the creation of 6,500 new affordable homes.

3. Bringing forward capital expenditure of up to £123.4 million for capital projects to help stimulate the construction industry in Wales.

4. £48 million secured for the ProAct scheme to help businesses retain staff faced with redundancy.

5. £35 million invested in the ReAct scheme helping those made redundant with re-training and re-employment.

Further to this, the Welsh Assembly government has:

1. ensured that European convergence funding is spent strategically to have maximum impact with greater emphasis on supporting business;

2. ensured that Wales is in a position to take full advantage of the additional £50 million funding for Objective 1 which was created by the fluctuation in the exchange rate with the euro – one of the few UK Objective 1 regions to do so;

3. created a fund totalling £20 million for apprenticeships focused on developing and training young people;

4. provided extra business rate relief, adding another 10,600 to the existing 37,000 smaller businesses across Wales that benefit from this scheme;

5. ensured that Finance Wales is providing commercial funding to growing small and medium enterprises throughout Wales and working with the European Investment Bank to create a new £150 million investment fund for small businesses;

6. established a £9.5 million Mortgage Rescue Scheme – becoming the first nation in the UK to take swift action to help those at risk of losing their homes;

7. made £600,000 available to allow credit unions, as responsible

lenders, to extend their financial services to the most vulnerable and to promote good financial advice enabling financial inclusion and financial literacy;

8. created a new £17 million initiative to provide training opportunities for students and graduates;

9. announced a £35 million investment initiative to help thousands of Welsh businesses turn their innovative ideas into cutting-edge products;

10. funded the 'Agile Workforce' scheme – a £12.5 million project to help tackle the difficulties that women face in the job market.

Plaid Cymru, as a party in government, is doing everything it can to learn from the mistakes of previous governments, to support the people of Wales through the crisis and to prepare for a more resilient future economy which promotes sustainable prosperity.

Because just as it wasn't Welsh companies, Welsh workers or politicians in Wales who caused the recession, the recovery will also have to be enacted in the main at a UK, European and global level. At a global level, free trade has to become fair trade based on certain minimum standards in labour and environmental regulation. We should, at the very least, insist on the kind of protection that our workers achieved at the beginning of the nineteenth century and, where possible, work with local NGOs, charities and trade unions to achieve progress. We will continue to work to end discrimination and worker exploitation through the adoption of stricter laws and improved workers' rights throughout Europe. In this vein, we have called for a strengthening of the Posted Workers' Directive at a European level.

We also call for a Europe-wide suspension of VAT on domestic gas and electricity for the next two years. At present, this tax stands at 5 per cent in the UK. We believe that it should be given zero per cent status during a two-year period to alleviate the problems of those affected by fuel poverty, a problem exacerbated by the current economic crisis with many, especially pensioners, having to make the invidious choice of either eating or heating their homes.

There is also a need for reform in the European rules which determine how Structural Funds are spent. Plaid Cymru in government will continue to call on the European Commission at this time to allow the Welsh Assembly government to increase intervention rates on structural funds and to allow an even greater degree of flexibility in enabling more help to be given to businesses to cope with the impact of the downturn.

The UK government should also call for a further temporary relaxation of some state aid rules to enable the government to provide direct support to businesses.

Given the indisputable role of the banks in contributing to this crisis and the impact on ordinary people and their wages, the culture of massive bonuses for bank executives has to be curbed. Bonuses for senior executives in any bank owned or part-owned by the state should be immediately banned until those institutions become profitable and socially responsible. Even at that point, they should be capped so that never again will city bosses be able to claim £19 billion in bonuses while wreaking havoc on the lives of ordinary savers. To ensure their robustness, these measures should be backed by legislation.

Spiralling executive salaries also needs to be brought under control. One of the main reasons for the growing wealth divide in the West has been the fact that business executives set their own pay. The law currently allows shareholders to vote on executive pay but these votes can be ignored by company boards. Democratising corporate governance and increasing shareholder power is the key to ending this abuse. Making worker, public sector and community representation on corporate boards mandatory, as is the case in other countries, could institutionalise responsible decision-making where pay is concerned. In addition, Plaid Cymru advocates the introduction of a statutory mechanism which maintains a balance between the amount paid to high earners within a company with that paid to ordinary members of staff, implementing a 'maximum wage'. Plaid further advocates a mechanism which prevents bonuses being based upon short-term results but instead establishes the principle that long-term growth and development should be financially rewarded and that these rewards should be shared among members of society and not concentrated in the hands of a privileged few.

Given the failures of the regulatory framework, Plaid is calling for a new social contract with banks including the creation of a new fund to further financial inclusion work within our communities which will be paid for by the banks. These banks will need to operate within stringent standard practices in relation to arrears, re-possession and lending. We support the FSA's banking code and its principle of treating customers fairly in order to ensure that lenders are held culpable if they lend money to individuals who are clearly not in a position to service incurred debt.

At an international level, Plaid will press for the introduction of a regulatory framework to control unbridled speculation by introducing a EU-wide ban on short selling. We will campaign for a global register for hedge funds including the US to achieve a level playing field for all financial players and also to ensure transparency and fairness. We will also regulate private equity firms and curb their ability to asset strip organisations that are solvent.

Plaid Cymru will encourage the creation of more regionally based banks and lending institutions and support the mutual model for personal finance and mortgages. We will further develop the work of the credit union movement in Wales and investigate the introduction of a low-interest banking network for savers throughout Wales via the credit union structure in order to promote a savings culture. To ensure that the people of Wales are better served by their financial institutions, we must explore the setting up of a national savings bank in Wales based on existing models from other European nations.

Although too early to judge the effects of President Obama's far-reaching programme for economic recovery, it is certain that the UK government's package has been neither bold nor successful so far. The stimulus from Downing Street needs to be far more ambitious. It needs to be judged by the extent to which it helps the unemployed poor, the working poor and those on fixed incomes too. In reality, the UK should have had a recovery programme five or six times the amount announced in the 2009 Pre-Budget Report in order to create a model with the same scale of ambition as the Obama Recovery and Reinvestment Plan focused on strengthening infrastructure.

Plaid Cymru believes that the UK government should introduce a stimulus package worth approximately £3 billion in Wales which will create and save 40,000 jobs between now and 2011. As in the USA, the plan should include a mix of measures including targeted tax cuts for low-income families and small businesses, special help for the vulnerable, extra cash to protect key public services like health, education and local government against budget cuts and a new green deal. This new green deal should invest in infrastructure, energy efficiency, micro-generation and the development of renewable energy to ensure that the environmental benefits will resonate for the rest of the twenty-first century as a positive legacy of the current economic downturn.

Plaid Cymru will also ensure that the necessary steps continue to be taken to commence 'work-skills' training among pupils from the age of fourteen and to ensure that educational and vocational courses are compatible with the needs of employers. An extra £32.5 million per year has already been made available to ensure this aim can be achieved.

Plaid Cymru in government will ensure the full implementation of the 'Green Jobs Strategy'. This strategy provides an opportunity for new jobs and wealth creation based on emerging and carbon efficient technologies. As the world's largest economies hopefully accept and come to terms with the emerging threats posed by climate change, Wales has to be ready to compete by taking advantage of the business opportunities that this could present.

There has already been a remarkable growth in the green technology sector in Wales over recent years which now accounts for around 9 per cent of the Welsh GDP. Plaid Cymru wants to ensure that the evolution in this sector can become a revolution in terms of its contribution to Welsh sustainable development. We will also pilot a project of free renewable micro-generation energy technology for those on low incomes with future energy savings shared equally between the government of Wales and the occupant over a 25-year period. Recognising the need to ensure that no-one is left behind in the green revolution, we also call for the creation of an EU funding programme to support deprived Welsh regions in making the transition to a low-carbon economy and society recognising the integral link between a strong economy and a sustainable community.

Given the challenges facing the public sector at this time of economic suffering, now is certainly not the time for the UK government to be planning severe cuts of potentially £500 million to the Welsh Assembly government's budget. This would have a devastating impact on Welsh frontline public services and Welsh jobs. Plaid Cymru will, at all levels, continue to put Wales first by demanding a fair financial settlement for our nation.

Furthermore, the UK government's plan to raise the National Insurance Contributions rate in 2011 is extremely ill-advised. It will act as a deterrent to employers taking on more people during a period of rising unemployment. At the local level, authorities should be encouraged to use their prudential borrowing powers to invest and stimulate local economies as well as using their own procurement policies to support and promote indigenous business where possible.

Plaid Cymru believes that the tax system should be genuinely progressive with those earning above £100,000 subject to a 50 per cent tax rate. We also call on the UK government to urgently raise capital gains tax to the same level as income tax in order to address the existing imbalance. There also needs to be an urgent re-think of the UK government's draconian welfare reform policies which will penalise the most vulnerable in our midst. Plaid Cymru is calling for an immediate root and branch review of benefits and tax credits aimed at creating a simpler universal system with entitlements set on sound economic and social bases.

We want to see the up-rate of benefit levels each year based on average earnings in order to sustain relative worth.

Recognising the integral link between the economy, unstable oil prices and the impact of rising energy costs on individuals, families and business, the UK government should also introduce:

- a cap on increases in energy prices, particularly for vulnerable groups so that people don't have to make the unenviable choice of deciding between either eating or heating their homes;
- a temporary, two-year reduction in VAT on electricity and fuel prices enabled by introducing a windfall tax on energy companies' profits;
- a fuel-stabilisation mechanism to ensure that individuals and families are protected from short-term fluctuations in the price of fuel.

As the economy falters and people face hardship and potential homelessness here in Wales, building on the success of our Mortgage Rescue Scheme, the Welsh Assembly government is working with housing associations and other organisations to purchase the homes of those facing the threat of re-possession and either re-let them or introduce shared ownership schemes. The potential cost to the public purse of not taking this course of action and seeing a steep rise in homelessness would be far worse.

The average property in Wales costs more than six times the average annual Welsh salary. Plaid is committed to ensuring that everyone has a right to an affordable home as an owner, part owner or as a tenant.

Other measures to avoid homelessness and ensure affordable housing are to provide grants for first-time buyers and provide local authorities with the ability to secure 100 per cent affordable housing on development sites, empowering them to control the conversion of full-time dwellings into second homes. Further, by promoting the expansion of Community Land Trusts, suspending the right to buy in areas of housing pressure and increasing the funding to support social housing, we aim to pursue policies which will help families in the midst of this crisis.

Plaid Cymru also wants the UK government to cut VAT on home repairs from 15 per cent to 5 per cent. In so doing, we achieve two key objectives:

1. We stimulate local employment and improve our stock of homes.
2. We create low-carbon housing and improve the insulation of homes thereby helping to address the challenges posed by climate change, ensuring energy efficiency and reducing energy costs for individual households.

Furthermore, the credit crunch has made it increasingly difficult for people to access mortgages as banks have taken a restrictive approach to lending. Plaid Cymru in government is exploring the potential of extending the role of local authority mortgages to provide a stable source of finance.

In terms of helping pensioners, in particular with the cost of living, the Welsh Assembly government will introduce a £100 discount to help with council tax payments.

Plaid Cymru believes that our objective must be to create the conditions to achieve and maintain an adequate standard of living and economic well being for all the people of Wales, in every part of Wales. We want to ensure that every young person in Wales has the prospect of securing a reasonable choice of job within their own community, have access to affordable housing and a wide-ranging choice of career opportunities within our country. Plaid Cymru believes that such aspirations should be secured on a basis that is environmentally, socially and culturally sustainable.

In order to achieve our aim, the Welsh economy must emerge from this recession in a strengthened, more viable position which allows it to compete more effectively, to become more enterprising, makes it less vulnerable in terms of its dependency on single sectors and also takes advantage of opportunities to develop a greener economic model. Plaid Cymru will call for action to be taken at all levels in order to deliver our vision of a renewed Welsh economy which is innovative, thriving and world-class.

The current global financial crisis proves that a Europe which promotes privatisation and deregulation is a Europe in which our post offices close, our communities decline and our banking services collapse in a flurry of irresponsible lending. Plaid Cymru wants to see a European-wide minimum state guarantee on savings of up to €150,000. If the banks are going to gamble with our money as indeed they have, there must be safety measures in place to ensure that ordinary savers do not suffer from their recklessness.

Plaid also believes that the banks should demonstrate a greater sense of responsibility towards their customers. To this end, we call for a Europe-wide tax on international banking transactions which would raise billions for meeting global challenges such as international development and climate change. Every time currency is traded across European borders by bankers, this Tobin tax would help to stabilise the volatile money markets, encourage accountability and promote responsibility in the banking sector. It is high time that the banks give something back to the people for whom they work. A tax on international banking transactions would raise billions for meeting global challenges such as international development and climate change.

For some time, Plaid Cymru has also been calling for a windfall tax on energy companies' profits: now we are calling on all EU member states to agree to make a concerted Europe-wide effort to tax the profits of these multi-billion pound businesses so that help can be given to people struggling with high gas and electricity bills.

Plaid Cymru believes that all governments (especially at the EU level), for both economic and environmental reasons, must support and encourage communities in their quest for sustainable food production and energy self-sufficiency wherever possible. There is great potential in Wales to localise our food systems, to promote our fresh, good-quality produce and to make use of our natural resources for green energy production.

We cannot, in the aftermath of this crisis, return to business as usual. We must introduce effective limits on leverage – how much financial institutions can borrow – and make irresponsible lending a criminal act. We used to have laws against usury and now we need a modern equivalent, setting a maximum rate of interest and banning the targeting of inappropriate levels of borrowing at vulnerable people. We also need a co-ordinated international effort to crack down on illegal tax havens. We should also end the tax loophole that allows hedge fund and private equity managers to claim their income as a capital gain, meaning they pay a lower rate in tax than those who work for them. Plaid appreciates the contribution of the voluntary sector, the third sector and the co-operative and social enterprise movement in Wales. We support the work that is underway in many communities aimed at ending social exclusion, the manifestations of poverty and the results of decades of educational and economic neglect. We want to work with voluntary organisations to improve access to rights advice and financial literacy. Furthermore, we will encourage local authorities to place free cash machines on council properties used by the public and to make reasonable access to free ATMs a condition when granting planning permission for new developments.

Over the longer term, the UK government should re-affirm its commitment to the pooling of economic sovereignty by making its inclusion in the European single currency an explicit goal of economic policy. Closer to home, improving transport links between major population centres across Wales by road, bus and rail has to be integral to any economic recovery plan for Wales. In government Plaid Cymru has, for the first time, announced a forward rail programme. It is also investing in improved bus services and is working to improve journey times by road and rail between North and South, as well as East and West. Plaid Cymru will continue to deliver on these commitments as part of its aim to spread prosperity across the nation. We will also develop sustainable travel within our towns and cities as well as between them with major investment in walking and cycling routes as well as public transport. Just as the Welsh Assembly government is bringing forward capital expenditure for projects, we will press at an UK level for a series of major public infrastructure projects in order to safeguard and create jobs in Wales. These should include the upgrading of the rail network between London and Swansea, initially through partial electrification and eventually adding a high-speed rail link and the electrification of the whole network.

We will also ensure that we invest more in the research and development capacity of our universities, stimulate and support innovation and commercialise new ideas so that the Welsh economy can become more sustainable, creative and cutting-edge.

Recognising that the economy of Wales is largely based around small-medium enterprises, often family firms or small businesses in a close-knit community, we will continue to assess the need to cut business rates further during the official recession in order to help sustain existing businesses and encourage further investment.

The rural economy

Plaid Cymru is committed to our rural communities. We believe that they need support to thrive, adapt and diversify to achieve a more prosperous future. For decades, rural Wales has been suffering from the same fundamental problems despite countless attempts to reverse the debilitating trends. These fundamental problems are:

- a stagnating economy that struggles to offer jobs or wages comparable to those available in urban areas of Wales or England;
- the drain this then has on the youth of rural Wales with the constant depletion of talented young people with the potential to develop rural Wales;
- mounting problems facing farmers in rural Wales with lower and falling prices for produce and increasing costs of production;
- housing – a major quandary that germinates from other problems such as lower wages, less stock on the market and external factors raising the average prices out of the reach of the locals and young 'first-time' buyers;
- increasing cost and operational difficulties in delivering services of all kinds, from schools and education to social and healthcare services given the sparsity of population.

Plaid Cymru has a proud history of developing policies to combat these problems. Plaid also recognises that public policy has shifted from agricultural production towards agri-environment measures. However, securing a sustainable food source for our country is becoming increasingly important, as we seek to lessen the carbon footprint of the food industry. Over the next few years, the agricultural industry deserves a period of stability. We will ensure that any transition to new support measures is as smooth as possible. We will work with farmers' representatives to secure a new scheme from 2012 onwards with the five existing agri-environment schemes being replaced by one scheme, Glastir. With the family farm at its centre, it is better positioned to meet current and future environmental challenges supporting a sustainable agricultural industry. Glastir will mark a major change. Farmers produce food and manage the land and they do so for their own commercial benefit and for the good of wider society. Glastir will pay farmers to manage the land in a way that will meet many of the priorities of today's society. We will also negotiate a fair deal with the European Commission for Welsh farmers.

Young farmers in particular deserve a start in the industry and there is an urgent need to lower the average age of farmers. In government, Plaid has introduced a scheme to support young entrants into the farming industry.

We will engage with all the relevant players to make sure that changes to the CAP and the support mechanisms for farmers post 2013 will not weaken our rural economy or damage the environmental gains which are essential for a thriving and sustainable countryside. As part of the One Wales government, Plaid is prioritising the following for rural Wales:

- Establishing a new entrants scheme to encourage and support young farmers into the sector.
- Developing an enhanced local food procurement initiative to get more local produce available in our schools and hospitals to tackle the problem of food miles.
- Introducing new measures to eradicate bovine TB.

- Developing a Rural Health Plan – ensuring fair access to health services for people living in our rural communities and who do not have the same transport networks as in more urban areas.

The commitment to the rural economy shows how Plaid wants to see a genuine regional economic policy with a more balanced approach to economic development. The need for a more diverse economic strategy should be central to the UK government's economic recovery plans rather than the current 'eggs in one basket' approach based upon the over-dominance of the City of London and the financial sector. The demand for the finite supply of housing in inner London could be addressed by re-launching regional policy and shifting whole government departments and entire institutions out of the South East of England.

In our view, a key component of a new approach by the UK government to economic development should be to allow devolved administrations to vary corporation tax rates in order to sustain and develop existing businesses, incentivise economic activity and attract inward investment. More than ever before, the current economic crisis also shows the need for the Welsh Assembly government to have borrowing powers so that a wider range of counter cyclical measures could be introduced.

In terms of stimulating growth in the production side of the economy, the UK government should consider appointing a Minister for Manufacturing within the Department for Business, Enterprise and Regulatory Reform. In order to help our important automotive and related components industry, Plaid supports the UK government giving cash incentives for individuals and families to trade in old cars for new, greener vehicles with the so-called scrappage scheme.

Why Vote Plaid?
Heledd Fychan (Montgomeryshire)

'To city dwellers, who occasionally visit the countryside of Wales on walking holidays and romantic getaways, rural life is idyllic. While warming up with a hearty meal made out of local produce in a pub, they'll often comment about the quality of the air and the greenness of everything and declare that they'd love to move to the countryside when the time comes to retire. And who can blame them? There is undoubtedly something magical about rural Wales – from the striking coastline to the dramatic mountains of Snowdonia – and you can't help but be impressed by its beauty

However, the truth is that, behind the scenes, day-to-day life can be tough for those living there day in day out. While the setting may be perfect, people face a number of problems – such as a lack of medical services, public transport, broadband services and even mobile phone reception. All these are things that are taken for granted of course by those living in large towns and cities. Also, long before the current recession, there is the issue of jobs. Agriculture used to be the backbone of many of these communities, and as times have changed, there are far less employment opportunities to keep young people within their communities. As a result, the population is getting older in rural Wales and there is a distinct lack of young families in some areas resulting in the closure of many rural schools, local shops and so on.

Plaid Cymru appreciates that there isn't a 'one size fits all' solution to suit every community in Wales. We may be a small nation, but our communities are hugely varied. Though there are some common problems, there are also unique problems requiring unique solutions. Plaid Cymru understands rural life, and that's why people in these areas tend to support the party. Our elected representatives and candidates have either been brought up in or lived in these communities, and appreciate the struggles and difficulties which are faced. They give a voice to those who are often ignored by the London-centric parties, and force rural issues onto the political agenda. They are also willing to implement tough measures when necessary to help combat those problems which are perhaps unique to rural Wales.

Nowhere has this been more apparent than in the Welsh Assembly government, since the Plaid Cymru Assembly Member for Ceredigion, Elin Jones, became Minister for Rural Affairs. She's displayed a thorough understanding of rural life, has mastered her portfolio and hasn't been afraid to take difficult decisions. This has earned her high praise among farmers, culminating with her being awarded the Farming Champions' Award in the Farmers Weekly Awards of 2009 because of her work in eradicating TB in cattle. Despite opposition from animal rights campaigners who are against the culling of badgers, Elin Jones has stuck to her guns regarding the policy and followed expert advice rather than pander to public reaction. Farmers love and respect her for this, and importantly to the party, it has reiterated to them that Plaid Cymru can and will deliver for rural Wales.'

There should be a greater emphasis on developing sustainable technologies by exploring with manufacturers opportunities to move forward with innovative technologies, such as fuel cells, which alleviate carbon dioxide emissions.

The need to skill and re-skill the workforce is essential if we are to maximise its potential and create a new Welsh economy. Following an assessment of their success, the Welsh Assembly government's pioneering ProAct and ReAct schemes should be rolled out as widely as possible with an emphasis on providing the necessary skills to supply our key, sustainable growth sectors.

Broadly, Plaid's economic thinking considers the need to recover, reform and renew Wales's economy. It sees how Wales has been affected by the global economic crisis and how the UK government's lack of decisive action has been in stark contrast to the Welsh Assembly government's rapid response. It looks at how existing policy must be changed and reformed at all levels from the local to the European to the international to ensure a stronger Welsh economy in the aftermath of the recession. Plaid believes that the renewal of Wales's economy, in the long-term, can only be premised upon a more integrated, more sustainable and greener economy in a vastly different global, regulatory framework.

Tackling the global climate crisis

As the previous section on recovering and renewing the economy suggests, it is impossible to divorce economic policy from its environmental consequences. The climate crisis facing the world has to be the most pressing political challenge that society faces and this should be the driving force behind policy initiatives and the urgency of action.

Reducing carbon emissions

The future of our planet depends on urgent action to reduce CO_2 emissions and adopt a different, more sustainable lifestyle. Plaid is committed to an annual carbon emission reduction target of 9 per cent. Plaid Cymru will continue to oppose the use of waste incinerators which might mean that people have no incentive to reduce and recycle, and which can pollute. Rather, Plaid believes in the waste hierarchy of 'reduce, re-use, recycle, restore and remove' and in strict waste prevention targets. In the European Parliament, Plaid has supported a recycling target of 50 per cent for municipal waste and a target of 70 per cent of construction and demolition waste by 2020. In addition, Plaid supports the idea of a higher landfill tax as a disincentive, to increase revenue and help to make alternative waste management methods viable and competitive. Plaid believes that there needs to be change to public procurement legislation in the European Parliament, so that local authorities and other public bodies can give preference to materials from recycled local sources, thus safeguarding the market and jobs created in this sector. Furthermore, as far as food production is concerned, Plaid Cymru is committed to enabling Welsh communities to build up resilience to potential food shortages which may arise as a result of the climate crisis, peak oil prices and reduced yields. Plaid believes that government at all levels must make more land available for use as allotments and community gardens, linking up with schools and other training providers to deliver local markets for communally grown produce. Our aim is to ensure all those who want access to land for food growing get it, and that traditional cooking and growing skills, which have been lost in recent years, are passed on to today's children.

As stated, one of our first priorities must be to reduce carbon emissions. Plaid believes that individuals, businesses and government must all change and alter their behaviour in order to reduce their carbon footprint. This holistic approach must cover everything from waste reduction initiatives, to supporting alternative means of transport to big-scale energy projects. Plaid supports emission performance standards for all new power stations. Plaid also believes that maintaining the existing housing stock can create many environmental opportunities and benefits. We support the removal of VAT from construction materials and energy saving equipment. We also call for a VAT reduction on housing renovation and renovation materials, since Wales' housing stock is older and is in dire need of renovation. Plaid also believes that since new build is VAT-free, this encourages new build rather than repair and renovation, which has negative environmental and behavioural effects. Plaid would like to see European funding for the development of a modern public transport system for Wales, with cheaper, faster railway links between north and south, mid-Wales and the west. In addition to the abolition of hidden subsidies for air travel, and the introduction of a fuel tax for aircraft fuel, Plaid wants to see an expansion in dedicated bus lanes and light rail in cities, with congestion charges where appropriate. We call for the improvement of commuter services in the Valleys and substantial transport improvements throughout Wales. Plaid Cymru believes that a green transport strategy must lead the way in a general attitudinal change across Europe. Linking 21st-century Wales to mainland Europe must be a priority in the coming months and years in the provision of better and more modern high-speed rail links and electrification throughout Wales.

Transport

Plaid Cymru has a vision for a modern all-Wales transport system that will unite the nation and promote more equitable economic prosperity. Building the transport infrastructure that Wales needs is a long-term task. Following the One Wales coalition agreement, Plaid leader Ieuan Wyn Jones AM has become Deputy Prime Minister and Economic Development and Transport Minister. As part of the One Wales government Plaid is prioritising:

- faster rail links between north and south Wales;
- substantial improvements on the A470 between the north and south of Wales;
- a more integrated approach to public transport;
- using a greater share of European funding on transport.

Ieuan Wyn Jones AM outlined his transport priorities for Wales announcing an increase in funding for improving the North-South links, which will mean an investment of significantly more than the £50 million pledged in the 'One Wales' coalition document. He also announced the following priorities:

- An enhanced TrawsCambria long-distance coach service between north and south Wales, with new routes and higher standards of service.
- A new Safe Routes in Communities programme.
- Doubling the level of European funding for sustainable transport projects under the EU Convergence Programme.

The Inn0v8 policies that formed part of our local government election manifesto in 2008 also outlined ways in which Plaid-run councils contribute to sustainable transport. These include:

- bike share schemes to reduce congestion on our roads, carbon emissions and promote a healthier lifestyle (such as the scheme recently introduced in Plaid-controlled Cardiff County Council);
- car share schemes to further reduce the traffic on our roads;
- greener buses to reduce the pollution that causes harm to our children.

Energy generation

As far as energy generation is concerned, Plaid believes that we need powers for the National Assembly for Wales over energy policy. In the first instance, society must alter its behaviour in order to reduce our energy usage as this is by far the easiest and cheapest way of making a difference to emissions. We also need the political will to give priority to investment in renewable energy. While Wales still depends on coal and gas and while there are reserves in Wales, Plaid supports the use of indigenous stocks rather than imports. Plaid wants to see further support given to research into technologies such as carbon sequestration and storage, fuel cells and more innovative technologies seeing Wales leading the way as far as research and development is concerned. Plaid is committed to an energy strategy which will create jobs and take full advantage of our natural resources. The energy sector in Wales at present accounts for almost 40 per cent of CO_2 emissions in Wales. European funding can be used to help re-structure the energy sector in Wales to make full use of microgeneration, tidal lagoons, small-scale hydroelectric schemes, seabed turbines and other sustainable energy generation schemes. We could support poorer regions to convert to a low-carbon economy and society. We have a plentiful supply of renewable energy sources such as tidal and wave power, hydro and biomass, which could also provide many opportunities for work and businesses. That is why Plaid Cymru calls for feed-in tariffs to encourage such small-scale renewable energy sources.

Green jobs

As previously indicated, we support the Green Jobs Strategy for Wales produced by the One Wales government in July 2009. This strategy provides opportunities for new jobs and wealth generation on the basis of new carbon-efficient technologies. In the hope that most of the world's major economies now accept the threat of climate change, Wales must be ready to compete and take advantage of the business and social enterprise opportunities which this may involve. There has already been substantial growth in the green technology sector in Wales over the last few years. Plaid in government is also initiating a pilot project for free micro-generation technology for those on low incomes, with future energy savings distributed equally between the Welsh Assembly government and the resident over twenty-five years. A long-term scheme to expand research and development, investing in new skills and training, and government support for small Welsh businesses would encourage an indigenous and innovative Welsh alternative energy industry. In recognition of our love for our land and our potential as a small nation to be agile, Plaid believes that Wales should lead the world in research and implementation of climate change technologies which will give everyone in Wales a more fulfilling and safe lifestyle, in a sustainable and responsible society.

Severn Barrage?

Plaid Cymru recognises that the environmental effect of a Cardiff–Weston barrage could be enormous. We call for European support for tidal power schemes in the Severn estuary which minimise environmental harm while at the same time generating low-carbon electricity at a price consumers can afford. Plaid believes there is potential to develop tidal power in the Severn Estuary in a faster, cheaper and more effective manner. A combination of tidal lagoons and tidal stream turbines will also mean less shipping movement through the area leading to an overarching positive environmental outcome. Plaid does not support the construction of any new nuclear stations in Wales.

Controlling our own resources

Plaid is totally committed to ensuring Welsh control over our energy resources and to the creation of a Sovereign Wealth Fund – we believe that Wales has been exploited in the past and that we must prevent this from happening again. Our natural resources must be used to generate real social benefits. Plaid believes that Wales's resources belong to Wales. If we are truly to create a sustainable nation, then our water and energy resources must be under our democratic control. For instance, we believe that non-contract water transfers from Wales to England should be carried out on a commercial basis, with the money being used to reduce water and sewage bills for Dŵr Cymru's domestic customers and to create community re-generation projects which promote equal opportunities, such as affordable houses in catchment areas where transfer schemes operate. In our opinion, it is ridiculous that the people of Wales cannot influence water policy. These clauses in the Government of Wales Act should be abolished. Water is an essential resource and should be treated as such.

Promoting a healthy nation

Plaid Cymru is committed to securing a healthier nation. Sixty years after the National Health Service was created, it's time to build a new health service fit for the twenty-first century. Plaid's vision is of health services rooted in the heart of our communities, a health service that is as much about promoting wellbeing as it is about tackling illness, a health service that will ensure that the people of Wales, whatever their background and wherever they live, have the opportunity to lead healthy and happy lives. Now is the time to invest in that healthy future. Already, Plaid has started delivering many of the health priorities it has advocated for years through the One Wales government. There are so many policy priorities, however, that cannot be implemented in full given the current weakness of the devolution settlement and so it is the case that there's plenty more work to do as far as health policy is concerned.

Plaid believes in a publicly funded, free National Health Service, not only as this is the most efficient way to deliver healthcare but also as it ensures that healthcare is available to all. Plaid believes in delivering appropriate services according to local need in order to best care for our communities, to sustain jobs in our communities and to ensure that our health and social services are sustainable and can realise their potential to improve the lives of all of us in Wales. As a party, we realise that health is as much about wellbeing as it is about illness. We recognise that we also need to look closely at the causes of ill-health; these include not only the long standing causes of poverty and unhealthy working and housing conditions, but also increasingly the misuse of alcohol and drugs, lack of opportunities to exercise, and exploitative marketing to young children. There are no quick fixes or miracle cures and this represents an enormous challenge ahead. However, a commitment to building a healthier nation is at the top of our list of priorities.

The National Health Service structures in Wales

Healthcare should be consistently provided across Wales, while taking into account the varied local needs of our communities. Decision-making regarding health and social services should be clear and easy for all the people of Wales to understand. The present structure is not securing an efficient, effective and understandable health and social services package for the people of Wales. A recent Plaid Wellbeing Commission argued that changes must be made to the current structures in order to secure a more accountable health and social services structure. Some of these changes are now being implemented by the One Wales government, with a reduction in the number of health boards.

Effective co-operation between local health boards and local authorities is of the utmost importance in securing the best possible care for our communities. Local health boards and local authorities social services departments should be required to share their budgets in the short-term in order to lower the numbers of delayed transfers of care. Such a move would facilitate an efficient system and could lead to an improved level of community care across Wales.

In 2004, out of hours services were introduced with the new GP contract; however, their quality, safety and impact on unscheduled admissions remains mostly unevaluated. Emergency admissions are particularly high in Wales and continue to increase. The reasons for this increase and the regional and local variation within it are also currently unexplored. Referrals from GPs represent the main route to scheduled care. These continue to rise. There is considerable variation in each of these trends by region, locality, local health boards and GP practice. The most appropriate nature and balance between areas for investment is yet again unknown. Data held by hospitals is incomplete and local health boards charged with planning services are caught in the trap of paying for services that NHS trusts data shows their patients have used. Clinicians have low levels of trust in the information as it is incomplete, and as a result it is not possible to project future demand. The lack of information on demand therefore places a stranglehold on drawing services out of hospitals and providing long-term planning for healthcare in Wales.

Secondary care

Plaid supports the re-configuration of health services as we recognise that, as part of a programme of improving services, change is inevitable. However, Plaid opposed recent proposals to cut hospital services the length and breadth of Wales as they contained little detail on how or where alternative services would be provided in the community. This lack of detail requires, as is mentioned in one response to the proposals, a 'leap of faith' from the public that community services will 'fall into place' alongside the closure of hospitals.

As noted previously, the acute sector in Wales currently absorbs an uneven amount of health resources, resulting in an imbalance in the system. Too often, too many patients are treated in the acute sector who could be treated elsewhere. Plaid led campaigns across communities in Wales in 2007 against the downgrading of community facilities on the basis that the plans responded to short-term financial pressure and failed to secure adequately planned community provision. Detailed, costed plans and timetables should have been put forward by every local health board explaining clearly how alternative community services would be provided following any re-configuration proposals put in place. Only by ensuring that adequate health services are available in every community in Wales can we ensure that balance begins to be restored in our health service.

A publicly funded community-based care service

Access to acute services will only be improved by providing greater emphasis on non-acute early intervention and preventative services. GPs under pressure at present can largely only refer patients to secondary care, putting severe strain on resources and adding to waiting lists. There is also growing concern regarding access to primary healthcare services in local communities across Wales. In Powys, concerns were raised regarding the lack of NHS dentists in the region, while in Rhondda Cynon Taf patients discussed having to wait three weeks for a GP appointment. Over 80 per cent of care is delivered at a community level, and yet the majority of funding is invested in secondary care. From the founding of the NHS in 1948 primary care such as GPs' surgeries and primary dental care has been provided almost exclusively by independent contractors and at present is commissioned by local health boards. While the services provided to the people of Wales have been of the highest standard, Plaid recognises that there are some areas in Wales where the provision of health advice and services to the community cannot be left solely to depend on the fortunate presence of sufficient numbers of independent contractors. We see clear examples of deprived and rural communities in Wales having difficulty attracting and retaining independent contractors. Plaid believes in the development of wellbeing centres where staff salaries would be publicly funded.

Wellbeing centres

About 30 per cent of patients who attend an A&E department could be seen elsewhere, while a quarter of GPs' time is spent on average dealing with minor ailments which require little or no medical attention. Wellbeing centres would be directly accountable in the first instance to the local health board. These healthcare centres would first be piloted in some of our most deprived rural and urban communities, communities where the traditional model of independent GP and dental contractors is failing to deliver. The needs of every community would be assessed and a multi-disciplinary team created specifically for each community. Services provided would not only include those of a GP but could include health care services provided by nurses, physiotherapists, counsellors and others. The pilot wellbeing centres would follow a co-operative model, ensuring that every member of the centre's team feel equal. Facilitating and empowering other health professions through the wellbeing centres would not only relieve GPs of their burden, but would also improve other health professionals' career expectations and job satisfaction. There needs to be recognition that each team member has a different, but equally important contribution to make to patients and their communities.

According to research by the World Health Organisation, chronic conditions will be a leading cause of disability by 2020. Statistics show that 38 per cent of the Welsh population have a long-term illness, and as a result 80 per cent of GP consultations are related to chronic conditions. Respiratory illness alone accounts for 28.5 per cent of visits by Welsh patients to their GP. Securing adequate primary care services in communities across Wales would also be a great aid in the long-term battle against chronic diseases such as asthma, diabetes, heart disease, and neurological conditions such as Parkinson's and multiple sclerosis. Targeting chronic conditions through disease management and prevention would be central to the work of the wellbeing centres. The wellbeing centres would also offer suitable and appropriate services for the community from specific health clinics on topics such as managing chronic illnesses like diabetes and asthma, to workshops on giving up smoking and leading a healthier life style. Such a scheme could create an incentive for dentists to train and work in areas suffering from severe shortages of NHS practitioners. Hand in hand with the Plaid proposal of introducing bursaries for students studying dentistry, such a scheme could seriously start to tackle the lack of NHS dentist services in rural and valleys areas.

A network of school nurses

Plaid believes in the urgent need to promote good health among children and young people particularly in light of rising mental and emotional health problems. The increase in the number of unplanned teenage pregnancies, sexually transmitted diseases among young people in Wales and the abuse of drugs and alcohol is also a matter of concern. School nurses are key in addressing these issues and ensuring that children and young people in Wales are healthy and happy. Their role needs to be restored and developed. At present, this field has relatively few nurses. There should be a minimum provision of one school nurse for every secondary school and its associated primary schools. This provision should first be provided in our most deprived communities, before being rolled out to communities across Wales. Often school nurses feel under valued and isolated from their nursing peers – a network of school nurses should therefore be based in the wellbeing centres. School nurses would then feel that there was a clear personal development plan and clear career options available by becoming a school nurse. By being based in the wellbeing centres their role and importance would be embedded in the community.

Mental health

One in four people in Wales will experience mental health problems. Mental health problems, however, are not often well understood and can carry a stigma that sometimes leads to discrimination and social exclusion and add further to the burden of illness. Living with a mental health problem therefore not only involves dealing with medical issues but also social, economic and cultural issues. Mental health services historically have had a Cinderella status and consequently have not always featured high on the priority list of commissioners and service planners. As a result, people with mental health problems have not always received the necessary access to specific services needed. Cooperation between health and social care, with associated lines of accountability, is crucial to supporting mental wellbeing and recovery. Despite long being a 'priority' for the previous Labour Assembly government, mental health services in Wales have been historically under-funded and lag far behind those in England. The promotion of mental wellbeing, enabling and empowering user groups and ensuring early access to a variety of services convenient to local communities are key to improving matters. These must be provided equitably to all parts of Wales, rural and urban. People in rural areas subject to proposed compulsory treatment through community orders should not be disadvantaged by having to travel unreasonable distances to access day facilities. Addressing the mental health needs of socially excluded and disadvantaged groups, particularly of black and minority ethnic communities, is also a priority.

Child and adolescent mental health strategy
One in five children in Wales has a mental health problem, and it is clear that child and adolescent mental health provision in Wales is in crisis. The service delivery proposals of September 2001 (as outlined in *Everybody's Business*, the previous Labour Assembly government's strategy for delivering child and adolescent mental health service issues) and the Children National Framework, to date, have received only minimal funding. At present Wales has an insufficient number of adolescent inpatient beds, fewer per head than the rest of the UK. As a result, children and young people have been placed unsuitably on adult wards, some a considerable distance away from their homes. Plaid is also concerned that 16–18-year-olds who do not attend full-time education cannot access children and adolescent mental health strategy services, especially given that adult mental health services are often inappropriate. We need to urgently consider a comprehensive resourcing of child and adolescent mental health and the national service framework for children and young people. We also recommend an end to the practice of placing children and young people on adult mental health wards.

Public health
In order to ensure a healthier nation it is vital to work within and outside the NHS. Policies that invest in our communities in areas such as housing and planning, transport, education, social deprivation and the environment are key to improving the health of our nation. Most of the factors that affect people's health lie outside their

control and outside the health service. Expecting individuals living under difficult circumstances to make healthy individual choices is unacceptable; people need clear, accessible opportunities to make different choices. Expanding the World Health Organisation's model of healthy schools to communities across Wales and further developing the Safe Routes to School programme could raise children's and young people's awareness of health issues. Ensuring workplace check-ups as part of a new requirement on employers to produce occupational health schemes could improve health in a working environment. Health and health service information (including new primary care data) should be collected and used to report independently on health status trends and on all non-health care factors affecting the wellbeing of the people and communities of Wales. This would be an important step in improving our public health as a nation. Plaid believes that there should be greater emphasis on ensuring that public health organisations in Wales are clear regarding their role and responsibilities. Plaid recommends using the World Health Organisation 1986 Ottawa Charter for Health Promotion as a guiding framework for the development and improvement of public health in Wales. The charter and its underlying themes, such as building healthy public policy and strengthening community action, are still relevant twenty years after its publication.

Free care

Plaid believes that older people in Wales should be able to lead healthy and fulfilled lives. Older people are valued members of society with a public role to play. We as a party aim to change the way older people are thought of in our society and we firmly oppose the unacceptable and inaccurate stereotyping of older people as dependent and infirm. The vast majority of older people are fit and healthy, but may need more attention from health and social service professionals to stay that way. Advancing years can bring with them particular needs in relation to care and it is an indicator of a civilised society that these are properly catered for. Older people deserve to enjoy their retirement to the full, and not in poverty. Disabled people should also be supported and enabled to live as independently as possible. Back in March 1999, The Royal Commission on Long-Term Care published their report on long-term care of older people and its funding. Little has been resolved since the publication of their report which recommended that in principle the cost of 'personal care' should be met by the state. By 'personal care' the Royal Commission meant both nursing care (provided by or under the direction of a registered nurse) and other intimate care such as bathing, feeding, dressing and help with medication. The Royal Commission also recommended, importantly, that intimate personal care provided within someone's home should be free of charge, following a thorough professional assessment.

As seen clearly in Scotland, free care can transform the lives of people who rely on support to maintain their independence. Free care can also avoid an intrusive and costly system of assessing general income and disability related expenditure. Ensuring that free care is provided across Wales could also end the postcode lottery that currently exists for charges and thus relieve the financial burden that this unfair system is causing many older and disabled people.

Plaid believes in securing free care provision in principle and as an aim. We reject the distinction between nursing and personal care. Intimate personal care cannot be described as optional or a matter of convenience for the patient. By linking entitlement to care given by nurses, the current funding structure puts providers before patients. It also leads to cases where older people are denied appropriate care, leading to health deterioration and often hospitalisation that could have been avoided.

We are also conscious that many older and disabled people are not aware of the benefits that they are entitled to, and therefore miss out on money that could improve the quality of their lives. The length and complexity of the application forms are often noted as barriers to claiming their entitled benefits. Stigma attached to receiving benefits is another barrier. As a party we condemn the unfairness of the means testing system. The system not only deprives people of their savings, but it is also extremely intrusive. Benefit 'take-up' teams should be placed in every local authority to advise and assist older and disabled people in particular in claiming their full benefit entitlement. Research by Plaid Cymru shows that every year over £860 million of benefits are not being claimed by those entitled to financial aid. Benefit take-up teams should first concentrate on ensuring that individuals across their local authority are receiving the disability living allowance and attendance allowance which they are entitled to and which should not be scrapped. Advice surgeries, home visits and targeting potential claimants would be a crucial part of the benefits take-up teams' work in making sure that older and disabled people can lead an independent life, and would enable older people and those with a disability to make a more significant contribution to local economies. This would be particularly important when new Westminster government proposals are implemented. Plaid believes that there should be a move towards free personal care through considering a new national care fund financed though a proportion of the revenue received by introducing the existing Plaid policy of replacing the current unfair council tax with a local income tax.

Plaid will carve out a distinctive health and social services policy which will re-build the NHS and keep within the principles of those who founded this vital service. Plaid believes that the people of Wales deserve health and social services that are clear, accountable and efficient. A national health service which will bring the health of our nation to the level of our counterparts in Europe is possible. It's therefore time to make that difference.

Educating the nation

Our children are our future. Plaid believes in laying strong foundations for our children and young people to succeed in life by implementing innovative and inspiring policies. Plaid believes that education is a fundamental right. Our children and young people must be equipped with the skills needed to thrive and everyone must have continued access to education and training to enhance their employment prospects and enrich their lives, especially at this time of economic crisis where adults have to re-assess their skill base. In this context, schools are at the heart of our communities, offering opportunities to all. The resources which our school buildings contain should be enhanced and made accessible to the communities they serve.

Educare, a scheme in which all care is educational and all education involves caring, will be the foundation of our policy in the early years. Through the early years curriculum, which emphasises learning through play, we are encouraging and stimulating those social and independent learning and living skills which will lay strong foundations for our children's development, supporting the pioneering Foundation Phase model of early years education.

Plaid believes in prioritising universal, affordable, and high-quality childcare, provided by a range of deliverers, for every family in Wales. High-quality childcare has proven educational benefits, giving children an early chance to develop important social and educational skills. Affordable and accessible childcare will provide economic benefits for families by enabling parents who wish to do so to return to the workplace. Universal, affordable childcare, available from the end of maternity leave, will also help close the gender pay gap in Wales.

Why vote Plaid?
Farida Aslam (Cardiff)

'A simple answer to this would be to say that if you are patriotic and love your country, your language and your culture and want to play an active part in helping your community prosper, then your natural choice in Wales would be to vote Plaid.

But to provide an understanding for those that have not thought in such terms before, we need to delve a little deeper and understand what motivated the founding fathers of Plaid. The philosophy that resulted in the Welsh nationalist movement and the party of Wales, Plaid Cymru, stemmed from the people themselves: their needs, and their rights. Plaid's foundingmembers were compelled by an enormous respect for the entire nation and the values held within its borders. These principles are embedded in the Plaid movement, which means it cannot and will not fail its people.

Looking at Plaid in practice and policy terms, as opposed to theoretical terms, it is clear to see how Plaid has kept its nation and people at the fore and developed some real ethical and principled policy positions. These include anti-war and anti-nuclear positions, a commitment to rural and economic development, affordable housing and the promotion of an ethical and sustainable green dimension that safeguardes our future while also addressing equality and inclusion for all.

Coupled with this, Plaid's vision of decentralist socialism means policies and decisions are to be made closer to home: in Wales for the people of Wales. This will not only reflect need, but also has the ability to make government responsive rather than time consuming and rigid, as is currently the case. Furthermore, the nationalism that Plaid promotes and aspires to involves the people of the nation, fully embracing their roles as equal citizens with a shared sense of belonging. It is a civic form of nationalism, valuing shared identity and inclusivity at its core. These principles will go some way to addressing the identity crisis and a sense of lack of belonging which exists across the whole of Britain's segregated Isles. Plaid's vision is one of a collective Wales: a Wales where all its communities prosper and play a part in the life of the nation.'

Plaid supports the goal of the elimination of child poverty in Wales by 2020. The employment opportunities for providers and beneficiaries and the better life prospects for children created by our expansion of affordable childcare will contribute to cutting child poverty levels. Access to information is vital in our increasingly IT-dependent world. The laptop is today's equivalent of the pencil and we owe it to our children to make available to them the medium of our time. Under a Plaid government, eleven year old pupils in pilot areas will be given their own lap-tops with the latest educational software, with the hope of making Wales one of the most computer-literate nations on the planet.

Plaid believes in replacing A-levels and GCSEs with a more broadly based baccalaureate. A Welsh Baccalaureate scheme will build on and learn from the current curriculum, but will be based on the renowned International Baccalaureate. A vocational as well as an academic form of the Welsh Baccalaureate will give students a genuine choice of qualification at fourteen. Under a Plaid government, education and training will be compulsory up to age eighteen for all those entering secondary school in 2008 (subject to enactment of the necessary legislation). This move is vital to tackle youth unemployment, improve workforce skill levels and equip the next generation for our rapidly changing society and economy.

Saturday schools for sport, music and the arts will be introduced on a pilot basis, as is the norm in other countries, as well as summer schools for students who fall behind in their studies.

Welsh medium education should be a choice for all in Wales, but the demand is not being met by current provision. Plaid will establish the right for all parents to choose Welsh medium education for their children. Plaid in government is creating a National Welsh Medium Education Strategy to develop effective provision from nursery through to further and higher education.

Plaid believes that pupils with special educational needs should have access to the provision they need to meet those needs in the language of choice on the basis of equality throughout Wales. We will ensure funding for equitable access to language and speech therapists. The ability of schools to serve children and their families successfully is wholly dependent on the commitment and hard work of Wales's teachers and support staff. Our aim when in government will be to provide teachers with the support and training they need in order to attain a genuinely professional status. Plaid will ensure that children are taught by qualified, registered teachers supported by classroom assistants. Plaid will create a clear training and career pathway for classroom assistants supported by a national pay frame. We will also guarantee a years teaching experience to all teachers who are newly qualified in Wales to ensure they can complete their induction year and become qualified registered teachers.

We believe there is an urgent need to promote good health among children and young people. A Plaid government will bring forward a comprehensive action plan to ensure that the children of Wales are healthier and fitter. A minimum provision of one school nurse for every secondary school and its associated primary schools will lay strong foundations for promoting good health from an early age. A school-based dental service will help address the tooth decay crisis among children and young people. We will pilot the introduction of free nutritious school meals for primary school children. This will help pupils to perform better academically and lay the basis for healthy eating habits. Plaid will seek a ban on the advertising of unhealthy food and drink on children's television and encourage schools to get rid of junk food vending machines. Free fruit at primary schools will help educate children's palates as well as delivering immediate health benefits.

Plaid believes in encouraging greater out-of-classroom learning, countryside and other outdoor activities, and increased walking and cycling to improve children's health and national wellbeing. We will direct more resources towards physical education and ending the sell-off of school playing fields and playgrounds.

Also, civic service in the community should be an integral part of the education curriculum. A new national citizens' service – a civilian equivalent of the TA – will be created for adult volunteers wishing to continue with civic service after completing their education.

Children in care are entitled to the same life opportunities as their peers. We will work to ensure that every school in Wales has a designated teacher for these children, and that a holistic and flexible education framework is in place for them. Plaid believes that all cared for children should have access to an independent and centrally funded advocacy service providing a reliable voice to speak on their behalf. Plaid also aims to ensure that leaving grants are standardised across Wales, offering young people the same opportunities wherever they live. Plaid further believes that local authorities should exercise responsibility for children in care until they are twenty-one years old, as well as contributing on their behalf to the Child Trust Fund.

As road accidents account for nearly half of all accidental injury fatalities in children, Plaid believes in increasing the number of 20mph zones in residential areas and 10mph zones outside schools during school hours, saving hundreds of Welsh children every year from death and injury. Plaid is also committed to improving safety on school buses.

Community and education are vital elements within our vision of Welsh society. We will therefore review the provision of community and lifelong learning opportunities and work to give communities a voice in the choice of courses offered in their areas.

Plaid will continue to oppose top-up fees at Welsh universities. In government, a decision has been taken to introduce top-up fees in Wales from 2010 onwards but upon Plaid's insistence, a scheme is being introduced to help tackle student debt and to encourage graduates to come back to Wales to live and work. So long as they have the acumen and the desire to enter higher education, our young people should be able to do so free of financial constraints. Plaid will identify necessary courses which cannot be studied in Wales, and seek to extend to students wishing to take those courses the financial support available to those studying in Wales. Welsh-medium provision in our universities is dependent on the goodwill and attitudes of departments, heads and lecturers, a situation we consider wholly unacceptable. The same is true in further education. There is a severe lack of educational provision available in Welsh and the present governance arrangements lack accountability. Plaid wants to see further education colleges more accountable to local education authorities with national terms and conditions for college lecturers. Plaid believes that a Welsh-language federal college should be established in order to secure progress on this important issue and Plaid in government is delivering the *coleg ffederal* so that students can access a wider range of courses in their mother tongue.

Schools are at the heart of our communities and must not be considered solely as buildings but rather as valuable community assets. We are committed to developing an integrated national education system for Wales reflecting our basic values and principles. This national framework would have de-centralised implementation and appropriation and would emphasise the values of co-operation, universal equality and fairness, social justice and social inclusion. The present market philosophy based on competition is divisive, inefficient and unfair. There is also a fundamental lack of transparency, equity and clarity in the funding system. Education is a service to the individual, the community and to wider society. Schools already play an important part in life long learning schemes. At the same moment, Plaid hopes to expand their role as a community resources. As far as our priorities are concerned, we need an education system which:

- introduces a more transparent, consistent, and visibly fair system of funding;
- promotes bilingualism;
- develops standards;
- builds national identity;
- educates children and young people on citizenship;

- enhances Wales's contribution to sustainable economic development;
- further promotes the good work of the 'Foundation Phase'.

Plaid Cymru-led local authorities look at creative ways for core services to use school resources. Herein, resources available in schools should be made accessible to the communities they serve. Plaid will ensure that local education authorities across Wales assess the demand for Welsh-medium education and produce a School Organisation Plan setting out clear steps to meet need. Plaid will campaign for local, wholesome and nutritious meals to be served in our schools, and commit to an increase in the amount spent on school meals to ensure healthier pupils. Plaid supports community and lifelong learning opportunities and works to give communities a voice in the choice of courses offered. We need to give our children the tools for success in the twenty-first century.

Tackling the causes of crime

Recognising that good health and education provided freely to everyone will give children and young people strong foundations and the best possible start in life, is part and parcel of our approach to tackling the root causes of crime.

Criminal justice policies are not working. The UK has the highest rate of imprisonment among all western European countries, with record numbers of children locked up. This is despite the fact that crime levels have fallen over the last ten years. Two thirds of prisoners go on to re-offend, while crime victim rates are 30 per cent higher than the European average. Levels of suicide, substance abuse and mental disorders are high among the UK prison population. Labour has adopted a shamelessly populist approach to crime in response to simplistic focus groups which tell them that crime is the voters' chief concern. Little regard has been paid to what works. We have seen a public campaign that has resulted in the demonisation of young people. In sum, successive UK governments have treated the symptoms of crime and not the causes. The One Wales programme of government, drawn up between Plaid Cymru and Labour, states that 'we want to see a fair system of youth and criminal justice, in which the people have every confidence' and that 'we will consider the evidence for the devolution of the Criminal Justice System'. Plaid believes in concentrating on the root causes of crime such as substance abuse, poverty, poor parental relationships, abuse and a lack of youth facilities.

Powers to deal with police, prisons, probation, the courts and sentencing should be devolved to Wales so that the Welsh Assembly government of the day can apply its chosen policies in those areas. The government's agenda would be implemented with the democratic mandate of the people of Wales. Under these circumstances, Plaid would pursue an alternative criminal justice strategy, focussing on tackling the causes of crime, reducing fear of crime and thereby making our communities safer. This strategy would include:

- freeing up resources to invest in public sector community rehabilitation and meaningful offending behaviour programmes in prison for those convicted of offences serious enough to warrant custody. The prison population could be reduced significantly with changes to sentencing policy to emphasise more community-based rehabilitation;

- the creation of a Welsh Youth Justice Board and consideration of the Finnish youth justice system as a model for Wales. Finland has a very small number of children in custody. Instead, there is a wide variety of psychiatric provision to deal with behavioural problems at an early stage;

- expanding social service departments to carry out more preventative work. Networks of child counsellors could be employed to work alongside an expanded Child and Adult Mental Health Service (CAMHS);

- replacing ASBOs with a system of restorative justice, mentoring and conferencing;
- a twenty year substance abuse strategy, focussing on harm reduction and including multidisciplinary substance abuse teams working with criminal justice agencies on individually designed care plans. Problematic substance users should be treated as patients. Primary school children should receive harm reduction education, with an emphasis on the promotion of mental well-being and suicide/self-harm prevention. There is also an urgent need for a wide-ranging public debate on the future of drug enforcement laws;
- a generational strategy to tackle hate or power-based crime. The primary school curriculum should contain 'relationships education' which aims to challenge and change early signs of sexist, racist, homophobic and bullying or abusive attitudes. It should also cover questions of sexual health, contraception and domestic abuse;
- protecting children from adult violence by putting an end to the defence of 'reasonable chastisement'. Adults convicted of smacking children in their care should be provided with training in parenting skills/social work intervention;
- a comprehensive strategy to reduce fear of crime through investment in facilities for young people, youth support workers and a citizens' public service scheme to bridge the gap between older and younger generations addressing the problem of some young people 'hanging around on street corners'.

What are safe communities?
As we know well, community life in Wales is at risk. The UK Labour government's attacks on public services and the historic lack of a

Welsh economic policy before the advent of devolution has meant that community viability has had to depend upon the whims of the market. While there have been some winners, most communities and the people living within them have lost out, especially in Wales. Safe communities can mean many things: from ensuring older, younger and ill members of the community are properly cared for; to anti-terrorist measures or to fixing paving stones. Safe communities are ones in which people can move around freely in public spaces, and in their own homes, without fear for their personal safety or the safety of those in their care. We cannot have safe communities unless we have active communities. For communities to be active, they need facilities – shops, pubs, post offices, schools, hospitals, social services and jobs, all acting as a hub for the community. They need to contain places where young people want to stay and go. They can become places that people with a contribution to make want to move to. Many of our communities in Wales are losing their young people, especially those who are highly skilled. As long as this 'brain drain' continues, these areas will become more deprived. Fear of crime is disproportionate to actual crime and existing government policy exacerbates this problem as it fails to address the causes of crime.

Of course, Plaid recognises that there is no one solution to dealing with crime. Criminal activity has existed since people have had laws, and it will continue for the foreseeable future. But it is clear that the current approach is failing. Why else would the UK have the highest rate of imprisonment among all Western European countries, some 50 per cent higher than comparative countries like France, Germany and Italy, and ten times more than Spain? And why would 72 per cent of the male adult prison population have two or more mental disorders?

Recent figures do show a decrease, October 2006 saw 3,350 children and young people locked up in England and Wales. However this figure has doubled over the last a decade. In another report, the

British Crime Survey (BCS), which asks young people themselves whether they have offended in the past twelve months (what is known as 'self-report methodology') shows that levels of crime have been static for the past five years. There has been a disproportionate increase in the numbers of girls and boys from black and minority ethnic backgrounds sent to prison. Two-thirds of adult prisoners re-offend, while a higher proportion of the youth prison population is repeatedly arrested after release, mainly for committing offences linked to a substance use problem. Nearly two-thirds of sentenced male prisoners and two-fifths of sentenced female prisoners admit to hazardous drinking, i.e. drinking that will affect one's mental and physical health in the long term. Of these, about half have a severe alcohol dependency (a physical and psychological dependence on alcohol). It is common for prisoners who have alcohol problems to also have drug problems. Just over a quarter of male prisoners and about a fifth of female prisoners who are hazardous drinkers are dependent on at least one type of illicit drug.

The women's prison population has doubled in the last decade. This rise in the female population can largely be attributed to the significant increase in the severity of sentences. For example, at the Crown Court in 1991, only 8 per cent of women convicted of motoring offences went to prison. That proportion had increased to 42 per cent by 2001. Similarly, women convicted of theft are now twice as likely to go to prison as they were in 1991. At the magistrates' court, the chances of a woman receiving a custodial sentence have increased sevenfold.

The majority of the female prison population is sentenced for non-violent offences. At the end of August 2006 the largest group (32 per cent) were sentenced for drug-related offences. More than two-thirds of women prisoners show symptoms of at least one neurotic disorder such as depression, anxiety or phobia. More than half are suffering from a personality disorder. Among the general population, less than one fifth of women suffer from these disorders.

The same people are recycled through the prison system, often on short sentences, making rehabilitation work difficult, if not impossible. Women in particular tend to serve very short sentences. For instance, in 2004, 64 per cent of women served custodial sentences of three months custody or less. Of the women released from prison in 2002, 65 per cent were re-convicted within two years of release. Short sentences lend very little time for prison and probation services to deal with emotional issues, drug addiction or education. At the same time, community penalties and drug rehabilitation requirements are underused for women offenders relative to male offenders.

Prison overcrowding means that prisoners are shipped far from their families and are therefore at a much greater risk of violence, riots and suicides and less likely to receive the rehabilitative support which will help them to 'go straight' on release. Plaid Cymru believes that the advent of primary legislative powers in the National Assembly for Wales must include the devolution of the Criminal Justice System, so that a more progressive approach to safer communities can begin across all levels of society, and so that such a programme is suited to Wales's distinct needs. Perhaps if this were the case, the north of Wales would finally have its own prison – a commitment which the UK Labour government has shamefully reneged upon.

The National Assembly for Wales has a significant impact on the crime prevention agenda in Wales, but its hands are tied by UK government policy on policing, criminal law, the courts, sentencing, probation and the prison systems. Plaid wants to see responsibility for all aspects of the criminal justice system in Wales devolved to Wales, including the ability to decide our own criminal law because Plaid believes that the most effective form of policing is the local bobby on the beat. The One Wales programme states that 'we will also consider the potential for devolution of some or all of the criminal justice system'. In the recent debate on the future structure of policing, our call for the devolution of police services gathered widespread support (if only mainly because the Home Office acted with such incompetence!).

In recent years, the Labour-run Home Office has presided over the largest ever UK prison population, increases in problematic substance use, a public campaign (in league with the tabloid press) which has made law and order a highly charged political issue, and the opening up of the probation service to privatisation. It has responded to tabloid scare stories of 'feral youth' by introducing Anti-Social Behaviour Orders (ASBOs) and the 'Respect' agenda. Drinking laws have been relaxed and super-casinos have been heavily promoted (even if they have rarely seen the light of day). New Labour has reduced civil liberties in a wide range of areas: clamping down on the rights of protestors; removing habeas corpus and paving the way for the introduction of a new surveillance and monitoring system for every citizen through the identity card scheme.

Plaid contends that New Labour has prioritised crime because focus groups simplistically tell them that it's the voters' main concern and it is a subject that readily attracts headlines. It has been a shamelessly populist approach. Crime has always been, and always will be, a chief political concern. Statistics show that since 1995 there has been a 42 per cent decrease in overall crime levels, while crisis point has been reached in the prison population with a 70 per cent increase since 1993. However, New Labour cannot claim the credit for this drop in crime rates. The UN Crime Prevention Agency's recent EU Crime and Safety Survey (2007) shows that despite falls in crime levels throughout Europe since 1995, UK crime rates have not dropped as fast as those across the rest of the EU. The UK is named alongside Ireland, Estonia, the Netherlands and Denmark as the crime hotspots of Europe, with crime victim rates that are at least 30 per cent higher than the EU average. The study concludes that no single factor can explain the drop in crime across Europe over the past ten years, but that a fall in the proportion of young males and improved security measures such as burglar and car alarms are probably more influential than tough sentencing policies or rising prison populations.

There are people living in communities in Wales whose behaviour is causing misery for others. In particular, behaviour termed as 'hate crime', such as homophobic or racial harassment targeted at minorities, can have devastating effects on the victims. So too can a small minority of young people whose behaviour intimidates, harasses and frightens people in their homes and communities. None of this is acceptable and it must be dealt with. New Labour has created over 700 new offences since 1997. People are being criminalised for things now that their parents and grandparents considered acceptable in days gone by. Children are now dealt with more harshly than adults. There appear to be numerous instances where incidents that used to be regarded as normal adolescent behaviour fifteen or twenty years ago are now being seen as low-level criminal activity. Young people are receiving ASBOs for playing football in the wrong place, playing loud music or making noise that disturbs their neighbours. They can receive a maximum of two reprimands (the equivalent of a caution), whereas adults can get an unlimited number.

We can add to that New Labour's obsession with appearing 'tough on crime', which results in more headline-grabbing measures to deal with the issue. The focus has been on low level, nuisance crimes, which have become known as 'anti-social behaviour'. This is a newly invented term. It didn't exist in our vocabulary until after 1997. The government claims that authorities receive 66,000 complaints of anti-social behaviour every day. If we accept that dealing with the causes of crime would be more beneficial than introducing ever-harsher penalties to treat the symptoms, then we must understand what causes people to behave in criminal ways.

What are the causes of crime?

The causes of crime are varied: poverty, substance abuse, a lack of youth provision and neglected mental health problems. It can be a combination of all these, or none of them. Bereavement or abuse can trigger problems that lead to criminal behaviour. It's also true to say that many people experience some or all of these things, but do not go on to offend. Plaid Cymru contends that New Labour's flawed 'Respect' agenda is also a cause of criminality.

Poverty

Young people are more likely to be seen on the streets in areas with higher deprivation, as there are fewer free or low-cost facilities. like youth groups, in such areas. Also, parents are less likely to be able to afford after school activities like music, sport or dance classes. Poverty brings difficult circumstances, hopelessness and in some cases fatalism. According to data from the Welsh National Database for Substance Misuse, the rate of referrals to treatment agencies for heroin use is nearly twice as high in Welsh coalfield areas as it is in non-coalfield areas, and almost one third more than in Wales as a whole. Poverty in Wales is a major issue. Of all the children in Wales, 28 per cent (162,000) live in poverty. The number is slowly reducing: it was 35 per cent in 1999, but poverty is still a strong indicator of possible criminality. According to Save the Children 56,000 children live in severe and persistent poverty. The 2006/07 British Crime Survey showed that people living in more deprived areas were more likely to be victims of crime than those living in less deprived areas; 10 per cent of households in the most employment-deprived areas had been a victim of one or more vehicle thefts, compared with 7 per cent of those in the least employment-deprived areas. In Wales, 640,000 people are living in poverty, 60,000 people are unemployed and a further 95,000 are 'economically inactive but wanting work'. Low pay is also a contributor to poverty. More than a third of poor households in Wales include an adult who is working.

Drugs

Problematic substance use is another key cause of criminal behaviour. There is wide availability of a variety of illegal and legal substances in every town in Wales. In 2005/06, 10.2 per cent of Welsh people aged 16–59 tried illegal drugs; 24.2 per cent of 15–16-year-olds smoked cigarettes weekly and 54.2 per cent drank alcohol on a weekly basis. The level of cocaine use is twice the average elsewhere in Europe apart from Spain. The use of cannabis attained record levels in the UK in 2008 but now appears to have stabilised, albeit at high levels. Cannabis use among young adults aged 15–34 in England and Wales still remains among the highest in Europe.

Solvent misuse (knowingly abusing a gas, vapour or solvent) is another area of concern. While much attention has been focused on deaths from illegal drugs, solvent misuse causes more deaths among young people aged 10–16 in England and Wales than Class A and other illegal drugs. In 2001, there were seventeen deaths from solvent misuse for this age group compared to five deaths from illegal drugs. In 2002, there were eighteen solvent abuse related deaths compared to six drug related deaths. Thirty-one young people aged 11–19 years and twenty-one people aged 20–34 died as a result of solvent misuse in 2002. Not all people who drink or use illegal drugs will develop what is termed 'problematic use'. Problematic use is when the use of a substance or substances causes problems in other areas of life, e.g. stops you going to work, makes you feel ill or causes you to commit crimes (most commonly theft or violence).

Lack of youth provision

Youth crime, as it mostly takes place in public, on the street, is the easiest to tackle. Although the Home Secretary has recently announced a review, government targets have been in place for 'offences brought to justice', where the police have to bring a total of 1.25 million cases to justice every year. Children and young people generally commit crimes in public places, in the streets where they are 'hanging around'. They are easy to catch and their cases are easy to process.

Young people are more likely to be on the streets if they have no alternative provision. Youth provision refers to the facilities and amenities that are available to young people in their communities. There are an estimated 4,046 youth clubs within Wales. Of these, 1,046 are public sector provision clubs and an estimated 3,000 are in the private and voluntary sectors. Many communities have no free or low-cost youth provision at all. A recent report by UNICEF found that children in the UK suffer greater deprivation, worse relationships with their parents and are exposed to more risks from alcohol, drugs and unsafe sex than those in any other wealthy country in the world.

Respect?

The 'Respect' agenda has been part of New Labour's discourse. A superficially attractive concept, the late Peter Clarke, the first Children's Commissioner for Wales criticised this agenda and pointed to the fact that the debate has been about young people allegedly disrespecting older people and not about engendering mutual respect between people of different generations. The UN Convention on the Rights of the Child states that custody should be the sentence of last resort for children. Yet twice as many children are locked up today compared to a decade ago. Youth and social workers are busy dealing with kids who have committed minor offences like breaking a window, meaning that their caseloads are full, leaving them unable to deal effectively with more serious behaviour, or with prison leavers. With only one secure children's home in Wales (at Hillside Centre, Neath), high prison numbers mean that children are being placed further away from their families and social workers, increasing the risk of self-harm and suicide. Approximately 84 per cent of young offenders from Wales are imprisoned in England.

Anti-social behaviour orders (ASBOs)

Although behaviour leading to the issuing of an ASBO is not a criminal offence, breaching the conditions of an ASBO is. Upon breach of an ASBO, people are being sent to prison for behaviour that was not serious enough to warrant a criminal conviction, let alone a prison sentence. Of all the ASBOs issued, 43 per cent are to under-eighteens. According to the British Institute for Brain Injured Children (BIBIC), 35 per cent of those have a diagnosed mental health problem or accepted learning difficulty. It is difficult if not impossible for some people to abide by conditions they don't fully understand. We don't know how many people have breached their ASBOs, as the data is not available, but a study by the Youth Justice Board in 2005 revealed that 700 children and young people had been imprisoned for breaching an ASBO.

A further study by the Policy Research Bureau and NACRO in areas in England and Wales found that almost half of the ASBOs issued to under-eighteens had been breached. Figures released by the National Audit Office in December 2006 estimate that 55 per cent of ASBOs have been breached.

ASBOs were introduced into British law in the 1998 Crime

and Disorder Act. After more than ten years, there is no evidence to show that ASBOs deter young people from committing or re-committing crimes or nuisance behaviour. In fact the opposite is true. Since 1999, MORI's work for the Youth Justice Board has tracked young people's experience of crime, both as offenders and as victims, indicating that offending levels remained static over the four years up to 2005. In many instances, failure to comply with an order is not simply due to a lack of respect, but is often more likely to be a result of the rigorous and often unrealistic demands laid out within the order itself.

Change for the better

It is clear that if we are serious about making our communities safer, we have to tackle the causes of crime and anti-social behaviour. Plaid Cymru has long advocated that the National Assembly for Wales should have powers over criminal justice in order to implement a safer communities strategy. Such a strategy would involve an overhaul of the criminal justice system to prioritise tackling the causes of crime. Plaid Cymru believes that a good place to start would be the creation of a Welsh Youth Justice Board, whose main aim will be to reduce the child prison population. The money saved should be invested in rehabilitation programmes and support. There should be further investigation and consideration of the youth justice system in Finland. A comparative analysis of the treatment of troubled young people in England and Wales and in Finland found that Finland has tiny numbers of young offenders locked up but accommodates 'very large numbers of children and young people in non-custodial residential institutions of one type or another'. These include reformatories, children's homes, youth homes and family group homes. By far the largest number – almost 4,000 – are held in special psychiatric units. If England and Wales had the same number of psychiatric beds per head of population as Finland, they would number approximately 40,000. In Wales, the Welsh Assembly government should exercise an overarching responsibility for every child, including those who offend or are deemed to be at risk of offending. We would ensure that teachers and other school staff are trained in a wide range of restorative and problem-solving techniques, which can resolve conflicts between pupils and between pupils and teachers. We should replace ASBOs with a system of restorative justice. If criminal acts have been committed then the perpetrator needs to be punished with criminal sanctions: probation, prison, fines, and community service.

Tackling substance use and its causes

Most crime is drug or alcohol related. Substance dependency and problematic use will be tackled by introducing a twenty-year substance use harm-reduction strategy. Investing in social services departments and specialist counselling services will enable the prevention of a significant amount of criminal behaviour. Adults with substance use problems will be able to access free counselling services and psychiatric support on demand. Alcopops will be heavily taxed and a strategy introduced to reduce youth alcohol intake. There needs to be substantial investment to ensure the widest range of detoxification and rehabilitation services are available to meet the range of substance users' needs. Crucially, problematic substance users will be treated as patients first. If they break the law to fund a habit, a properly funded public probation service should work with other agencies to implement a personal plan to avoid offending including, where appropriate, the use of substitute medication. This plan could be implemented in prison, where necessary.

The One Wales government is committed to allowing the prescription of diamorphine (medical grade heroin) under strictly supervised medical conditions, if the pilot currently underway in England proves to be a success. To reduce crime, we believe in the introduction of multi-agency substance treatment centres, where problems can be dealt with by a range of professionals all working together in the same building. The UK's 35-year war against illegal drugs is lost. A public debate on the future of drugs laws is overdue. Attempts to reduce the supply of drugs into the UK have failed. The price of all illegal drugs has lowered, showing higher levels of availability. Currently around 70 per cent of the total UK drugs budget is spent on enforcement. Approximately 20 per cent is spent on health, and 10 per cent on education. This expenditure needs to be re-prioritised to concentrate on tackling the causes of substance problems. If we could accept that some people are going to use substances, then we could focus public spending and energies on those whose use either causes problems for others, e.g. through violence or burglaries, or those whose use is causing problems for themselves and others such as substance misusing pregnant women. The aim of a harm reduction strategy would be to reduce the risk of harm to individuals and communities. To this end needle exchange schemes should be promoted, as well as safe injecting facilities and other harm reduction measures.

Rehabilitation to reduce re-offending
The probation service has 13 per cent lower re-offending rates than prison. This is despite severe budget cut backs, out-sourcing and staff shortages in the service in recent years. Probation officers and youth offending officers already deploy a wide range of programmes that have a proven effect in reducing the risk of criminality. The money saved by reducing the prison population will be re-directed to make sure that rehabilitation workers have manageable caseloads and can carry out their work effectively. Plaid Cymru wants to reverse any legislation that opens up offender rehabilitation work to the market

in Wales. We recognise that prison will be an inevitable outcome for some offenders. Prisoners should be entitled to a basic minimum standard of health, education, rehabilitation and re-settlement services while serving their sentences and on release. Each prisoner should have an individual offending behaviour reduction plan aimed at avoiding future incarceration.

We believe that the measures outlined above will reduce actual levels of crime in the long term. Particular measures are needed to tackle the fear of crime that exists today. An Assembly government without devolved criminal justice services could still introduce a strategy to reduce fear of crime. It is vital that young people are involved in local forums designed to tackle this issue. Their ideas for combating problematic behaviour will be invaluable. Crime hot-spots could see increased police visibility, if appropriate, but more use of outreach youth workers and increased free or low-cost youth provision will be encouraged. Plaid wants to see investment in a wide variety of youth provision. For example, a citizens public service scheme helping young people develop a sense of public service and responsibility. At the same time, such a scheme could help to provide a bridge between young and older generations, which will further reduce the fear of crime in the long term.

Living in cohesive communities

Another policy area which has suffered from the lack of a real and meaningful debate in a Welsh context is that of immigration and what it means to live in a cohesive community where the majority of people get on. The left, including Plaid Cymru, is often scared of this subject, worried that even talking about the issue will lead to charges of racism. This often means that the subject is the prized possession of the extreme right who, in the absence of an alternative viewpoint, peddle their extremist lies and get away with it. This lack of confidence in talking about immigration among the left means that genuine abuse of the migration system becomes the sole preserve of the extreme right, who use this in a casual way to prove that their racist diatribe about so-called 'bogus', 'cheating' migrants is consequently true. As we know well in Wales, immigration is a reality of politics, contemporary and old. Millions of people uproot themselves from their established communities either voluntarily or out of necessity in order to seek a better life or to escape persecution be it temporarily or permanently. A quick glance over early Census inserts in the Cardiff dock area confirms that people have been moving in and out of Wales for centuries.

Migration is therefore a term that can encompass the movement of individuals and people across established country borders in many diverse ways. In this sense, it can be a policy area that includes asylum, refugee issues, economic migration, EU A8 accession migration (that is, migration from those countries which joined the European Union in 2004), EU A2 accession migration (that is, migration from those countries which joined the European Union in 2007), non-EU immigration, in-migration from England to Wales, the brain-drain to England from Wales and so on.

Plaid recognises that correlating immigration politics with racism in itself does not answer legitimate questions around migration and also acknowledges a need to 'say more' than simply 'Plaid Cymru believes in sustainable, cohesive communities where discrimination is abhorred'. This should, of course, be a given.

Plaid Cymru believes in a strong, sustainable and cohesive Wales where everyone is valued. Wales's people are united in their diversity and are welcoming of those who come here to work and live. Plaid Cymru believes that Wales is a country where each and every individual is respected and valued irrespective of their race, language, nationality, gender, colour, creed, sexuality, age, ability or social background. Those who migrate to Wales from

A8 accession countries (the 2004 EU accession countries) mainly come from Poland and Lithuania and do so for economic reasons. They account for the highest number of migrants into Wales (bar those who come to Wales from elsewhere in the UK). EU A8 accession migrants are not asylum seekers. Most A8 migrants are economic migrants helping to fill gaps in our national labour market, particularly in administration, hospitality, tourism and the care sector, which are important industries vital to the well-being of the people of Wales. Unlike asylum seekers who are dispersed to Cardiff, Swansea, Newport and Wrexham upon arrival in the UK, economic migrants from the EU are free to live in a place of their choosing and often live in fairly remote, rural communities. There are older established communities of migrants from these countries already living in Wales since after the Second World War (such as in Pwllheli).

Many people don't understand the differences between the various types of migrants listed above. The extreme right and the tabloid London-based press exploit this ignorance suggesting that the UK is 'swamped', that 'bogus asylum seekers' or 'fake migrants' are here to cash in on an apparently soft state and that millions of young men in poorer economies in the emerging EU are poised to enter the UK to 'steal jobs'. Their underlying motivation is racism and xenophobia.

As Plaid's Adam Price MP recently said: 'we need more information and an honest discussion about migrant workers if the left is not going to yield ground to the extreme right'.

Plaid Cymru believes that we in Wales can propose our own solutions to the problems of migration: particularly in the context of EU migration. Here, we aim to make sure that immigration has a positive economic effect by implementing robust policy in order to manage the situation properly.

Underground economy and exploitation

Many economic migrants are being signed up in their mother countries by UK-based employment agencies and are tied into housing and transport-to-work arrangements which see these costs deducted from their pay. This is a convenient way for profiteering bosses to undercut the minimum wage, creating cheap labour and therefore creating a skewed market which favours migrants at the expense of host country workers or local communities. Further, from a social welfare point of view, these migrants are often crammed into over-crowded accommodation where beds are shared in shifts creating unacceptable living conditions for the workers themselves. The workers are often bound to these contracts before they arrive in Wales. This exploitation and trafficking of cheap labour is unacceptable and should not be tolerated.

Lack of resources for local authorities

Due to the Home Office's inability to keep track on figures and recent controversy over different government departments releasing different figures, local authorities often have no clear information of the needs of new emerging communities or the pressure on existing service areas such as housing or education. If a number of children present themselves in a school with no support for speakers of a language other than Welsh or English, in areas of Wales which have very little experience of teaching in a different language, then this cannot be good for the school or the pupils. Local authorities need information in order to forward plan, especially given that the debate on capping numbers of migrants is wholly irrelevant given that Wales, via the UK, is part of the EU common market.

Gangmasters' Licensing Authority

At present, the Gangmasters' Licensing Authority has no

permanent office or offices in Wales despite the increasing number of economic migrants employed in various industries in both urban and rural Wales. Further, the current remit of the GLA is limited to a small number of sectors and does not for instance include the construction and retail industries.

People trafficking
The Home Secretary's recent decision to slash the funding available for specialist policing is wrong. People trafficking is a growing crime and has to be treated in the same way as other organised crimes like drug smuggling.

Where we could be – Plaid policy proposals
1. Minimum wage – no cuts. Plaid Cymru believes that a Fair Employment Bill would go a long way to curb the exploitation of economic migrants. It could include, for instance, equal working conditions for migrant workers along with the extension of the Gangmasters Licensing Authority through the Gangmasters' Act to also include areas that are not presently covered (like construction and retail). There should be specific attention to the current practice of docking wages to create cheap labour as this effectively means the cutting of the minimum wage. If anything, the minimum wage should be increased in order to ensure that economic migrants are not a cheap source of labour purely there to increase the profit margins of unscrupulous employers. By ending the exploitation of economic migrant workers by unscrupulous agencies and gangmasters, the skewing of the market and the creation of underground economies could be addressed, resulting in a migration equilibrium.

2. Accuracy of figures – recognition of role played by local authorities. Local authorities need support and guidance, based on accurate figures, to ensure that their budgets are appropriate and that resources are channelled to help children integrate into local schools and to ensure that migrants have access to key public services such as the NHS. Data from various sources, like GP surgeries, should be collated. Without accurate figures, the extreme right can seize upon sensationalist headlines to further suggest that Wales is being swamped.

3. Gangmasters Licensing Authority: remit widened/office in Wales. The Gangmasters' Licensing Authority currently has no office in Wales. Not only should its remit be widened but it should also have a presence in Wales to ensure that the exploitation of workers is tackled at root.

4. People trafficking: restoring proper funding to police. The Home Secretary should reverse a recent decision to cut funding, follow the lead of the One Wales government in funding the policing of trafficking, and honour the UK's commitments under the European Convention on People Trafficking by supporting this specialist police team.

Talking of introducing caps is nonsense in a Europe where we value the free movement of people. In a globalised economy, the migration of workers is inevitable. As people in Wales, we value the right to work abroad in a European country – it's a two-way street. Limits and caps are unrealistic. We need people to work in our underfilled job sectors: Wales has an ageing population (35 per cent of population is retired) and nearly a third of key workers in the NHS were not born in the UK. The culture of exploitation where people are being exploited to increase profit margins – worthy of Victorian Wales – needs to end. The real urgency lies in putting an end to discrimination and exploitation through tighter legislation and improved living standards. It's clear that the many people who move to Wales make a rich contribution to quality of life in Wales and often sustain sectors – such as the care sector – which look after the most vulnerable. None of us have to look too far back into our own family histories to find grandparents and great grandparents who've uprooted themselves to seek a better life. We believe that migrants should not be the scapegoats for the failures of government to tackle poverty and social injustices. The provision of social housing and decent jobs and pay is the duty of the government and the failure of the UK government to protect workers' rights should not be obscured by a debate about immigration.

Fair funding for Wales

Plaid Cymru wants to establish a strong sustainable basis for a thriving nation and we will not take a short-term approach to governing or financing Wales. Plaid has campaigned strongly for a fairer funding formula geared to giving Wales the investment and services it needs. Plaid has long argued that under the status quo, Wales has been losing out on billions in funding for front-line public services such as health and education. This matters because Plaid believes that Wales has always lost out in the asymmetrical, unjust British state and that for as long as Wales remains a constituent nation of the UK state, it must be adequately financed. Anything less is simply a disgrace. Wales, for much of the twentieth century, has experienced economic decline compared with the rest of the UK. This was principally a consequence of the decline in traditional manufacturing or producing industries such as coal, steel, agriculture and slate quarrying. Wales has been funded through a block grant allocation distributed under the Barnett formula introduced in 1980. The formula, introduced only as a temporary measure, takes no account of the disproportionate impact that this decline has had on Wales compared with the rest of the UK and the current funding formula not only reflects the spending needs and priorities of England, but seeks to converge funding per capita across then four countries of the UK irrespective of the differing and diverging needs.

In designing a funding mechanism for the countries of the UK, a set of principles needs to be established. These principles should be:

- that funds available should be related not only to need but to remediation of disadvantage;
- that the Assembly government should have some tax varying powers;
- that the Assembly government should have borrowing powers;
- that the forum in which decisions are made regarding the allocation of funding to the four countries of the UK will afford devolved government administrations a key say in the decision-making process.

Plaid believes that the Barnett formula is both unfair and unsatisfactory and should be replaced. A new set of proposals should be designed to remedy to current situation and enable a more satisfactory system involving the establishment of an independent funding commission. Some fiscal powers should be granted to the Welsh Assembly government which at present has responsibility for the expenditure of the block grant but has no responsibility for its size. This lack of accountability is a key weakness and the provision of tax varying powers would improve accountability and focus more attention on wealth creation in Wales. As part of fiscal devolution the Assembly government should have borrowing powers within a prudential borrowing framework. Such a step would facilitate the planning and management of capital investment in Wales.

To facilitate both borrowing powers and the ability to assume contingent liabilities the funding arrangements for the Welsh Assembly government should be put on a statutory basis.

Plaid Cymru has a long record of opposition to the Barnett formula and welcomed the commitment of the Assembly government, as part of the One Wales coalition agreement, to establish a commission to review the funding and financing arrangements for Wales. In economic terms Wales has long been a relatively poor country compared with other parts of the UK. The reasons for this are complex. Wales was slow to urbanise; was very dependent on an agricultural sector which suffered from a high proportion of poor-quality land with low productivity; when industrialisation came, it was concentrated initially on extractive industries with much of the added value being contributed elsewhere. Viewed from a UK perspective such specialisation may have made sense but it left Wales with an economy highly dependent on a few business sectors all of which suffered long term decline over much of the twentieth century (agriculture, coal, steel and slate quarrying). Although the Assembly government is now making considerable efforts to strengthen and diversify the Welsh economy, most of the significant levers remain in the hands of Whitehall.

Wales now has the challenge of dealing with this legacy, but during much of the last hundred years or more UK governments have regarded Wales as being on the periphery and have sought at best to ameliorate economic weakness rather than address the root causes. Since the implementation of the Barnett formula, which takes no account of relative need, GVA per capita has declined from 88 per cent of the UK average in 1978 to 75 per cent in 2007. The way successive UK governments have viewed Wales is reflected in the way that devolved services are funded: in particular, both the formulation and operation of the Barnett formula reflect the peripheral status of Wales. Changes to the block grant are a *consequence* of spending decisions made with respect to spending departments in England. Indeed, as is noted in the Treasury's

Statement of Funding Policy, in the vast majority of cases, the United Kingdom departmental programme covers England only and yet it is decisions made by such departments that drive changes to the funding of Wales.

Out of UK total managed expenditure (TME) for 2007/08, of £590 billion, the UK government was directly responsible for:

- non-identifiable expenditure for the UK (£108 billion). This encompasses defence, interest on the national debt, cost of central government etc;
- social Security (£156 billion) which is a standard, needs-related UK wide set of programmes;
- identifiable but non-devolved expenditure in Scotland, Wales and Northern Ireland (£3 billion);
- all public expenditure in England (£243 billion) excluding locally financed expenditure.

The devolved governments and local authorities of Scotland, Northern Ireland and Wales had responsibility for £60 billion of expenditure. Thus essentially the UK government is, from a financial viewpoint, responsible for all public expenditure associated with the UK per se (central government expenditure including social security) and for all public expenditure in England. Further, it is responsible for a very small amount of spending on non-devolved, identifiable expenditure in the other three countries of the UK (£3 billion) which is less than 0.5 per cent of TME. In addition the UK government is responsible for fiscal policy i.e. setting and collecting all taxes and duties in the UK with the exception of council tax and business rates. A third financial role is that the UK government is responsible for macroeconomic policy including the setting of overall public expenditure levels in the UK and determining the level of public sector indebtednesses.

Guiding principles

In reviewing the funding and financial arrangements for Wales, Plaid believes that certain principles should be agreed:

- The funds available should be related not only to need but also to the remediation of disadvantage. Funding should be sufficient to enable the devolved administrations to address the underlying causes of any relative underperformance of the economy and its consequential social impact.
- The Assembly government should have tax-varying powers.
- The Assembly government should have borrowing powers.
- The forum in which decisions are made regarding the allocation of funding to the UK and to its four member countries should be such that the governments of the devolved administrations have a key say in such decisions.
- The conflicting position of the UK government in its dual role as the government of the UK and of one of the four member countries of the UK should be recognised.

It is not sufficient to set funding levels in terms of relative need. Plaid believes that it should be the objective of the UK government to ensure that the devolved administrations have the means to address and materially reduce economic and social disparities between the member countries of the UK. The present funding arrangements appear, at best, designed to ameliorate the effects of economic and social disadvantage. It is noteworthy that in recent times the UK government has to a marked extent abdicated to the EU its responsibility for the additional funding of disadvantaged areas. Even in the case of EU funding the UK government hesitated initially to pass onto Wales the EU Objective 1 funding.

It is clear from the above that Plaid Cymru considers the current funding formula to be both unfair and unsatisfactory. We believe that a number of steps to reform it are necessary and that eventually the current formula must be replaced. The first three steps proposed would be simple to implement but would not address the key weaknesses of the Barnett formula. A useful first step, albeit a modest one, would be more clearly to identify, within government reporting, expenditure by Whitehall departments which is for those services in England which in the case of the other three countries of the UK are devolved. This would enhance transparency and facilitate comparisons between the member countries of the UK. A second step would be for the National Audit Office and the Wales Audit Office to review and report annually to Parliament and the National Assembly, respectively, on the operation of the Barnett formula. A third step would be to stop the Barnett squeeze by increasing the block grant to Wales by the same percentage as the corresponding increase in expenditure in England. In the absence of evidence to the contrary there is no justification for arbitrarily reducing relative identifiable public expenditure per capita on devolved services in Wales. Such a change would be a trivial modification to the current Barnett formula and would not increase total managed expenditure. A fourth step would be to apply the principle that relative funding of services in the four countries of the UK should be related to relative need as is the case for intra-country distribution of funding. Determination of relative need is of course a complex and potentially contentious subject. Given that expenditure on devolved public services is concentrated on health and education (approximately 70 per cent of the total) it is possible to formulate an acceptable needs model. Assessment of need is a challenge not unique to the UK and the Funding Commission should consider models employed in other countries with varying degrees of devolution. The additional funding needed to address remediation would be over and above the needs requirement.

Devolution of fiscal powers

Another important step is for some fiscal powers to be devolved to Wales. A first stage would be to allocate all or some of the yield of certain taxes to Wales and then for the Assembly government to have the power to set, in whole or in part, the rate of those taxes. This would be a desirable change because, for the first time, the Welsh Assembly government would start to concern itself with income as well as expenditure: a vital connection if the Welsh Assembly government is to be more accountable for the country's economic success and overall well-being. An important principle is that the block grant to the National Assembly should be unaffected by any variation to tax made by the Assembly government.

In principle, it is important that the Welsh Assembly government has a measure of control over a number of different taxes rather than being reliant on one or two only. This is to ensure that the tax base is sufficiently wide and that action taken by the UK government with respect to any one tax does not have too adverse an effect on the position in Wales. For example, if Wales were to receive funds arising from income tax only, then a decision made by the UK government to reduce dependency on income tax and move the tax burden to indirect taxes could have an immediate and deleterious impact on revenues assigned to Wales. This would argue in favour of Wales being assigned some or all of the income arising from a number of the most widely based taxes such as income tax and value added tax. This would mirror to some extent the arrangements in Germany for example.

In 2006/07 identifiable public expenditure in Wales by the Welsh Assembly government and local authorities totalled £15.2 billion. Oxford Economics has estimated that in the same year, total tax receipts that can be allocated to Wales were £19.3 billion including £4.7 billion from income tax, £3.6 billion from national insurance contributions and £3.2 billion from VAT. Thus taxes that can be allocated to Wales more than cover the total current budget of the Assembly government.

Furthermore mechanisms for allocating these taxes should be fairly straightforward (the annual *Budget Red Book* published by the Treasury now includes an estimate of the yield to Scotland if income tax were varied by 3p). In the case of taxes such as corporation tax the position is more complex but nevertheless worthy of further consideration for economic development reasons.

An important principle is that if tax varying powers are employed by the Assembly government in the shorter term the block grant should not suffer a corresponding increase or decrease making the devolution of fiscal powers self-defeating.

In the short to medium term, social protection should continue to be a UK wide programme with citizens being treated according to need in all parts of the UK. This reflects the common practice in many other unitary and federal states which have devolved government.

Borrowing powers

As part of a move to fiscal devolution, the Assembly government should have borrowing powers within a prudential borrowing framework. After all, local authorities already have such borrowing powers although their revenue raising powers are extremely limited. The Assembly government should be able to raise money in the capital markets in a similar way to devolved administrations in other parts of the world. The rating agencies would take a view as to the credit worthiness of any such issuance of debt and this, in turn, would constrain the Assembly government to prudent borrowing. In practice it is probable that the UK government would wish to set further constraints or limits and this should be on the basis of the Assembly government being able to have borrowing limits in line with its proportion of total UK public expenditure.

There is also potential for the Assembly government to use its ability to assume contingent liabilities up to the value of the block grant. This enables it to provide guarantees to third parties under certain circumstances and could be used for funding of capital investment in the public sector. In the case of borrowing powers and contingent liabilities it would greatly facilitate matters if the funding of the Assembly government were placed on a statutory basis: this should be done.

Plaid Cymru believes that the current funding arrangements for Wales are both unsatisfactory and unsustainable and should be replaced. Wales has suffered for far too long in terms of inadequate and unfair funding. The funding, borrowing and fiscal measures advocated in this paper would both lead to a fairer allocation of funds and ensure that the Welsh Assembly government assumes increasing responsibility and accountability for the economic and social success of Wales.

Creating a safer world

At present, two key issues dominate international policy: Iraq (in particular its subsequent inquiry) and the war in Afghanistan.

Plaid opposed the illegal war in Iraq, leading a campaign to impeach then Prime Minister Tony Blair for misleading Parliament in relation to his assurances over WMD. This position has been more than vindicated given Blair's comments that even if there were no WMD present in Iraq, he would still have gone to war: thus showing a complete contempt for the troops who lost their lives, the hundreds of thousands of innocent Iraqis killed and total disregard for international legal agreements on conflict and peace. Plaid opposes the war in Afghanistan believing it is a war that can never be won. Plaid has been the only political party in mainstream UK politics to oppose both wars even at times when this has been politically unpopular. Plaid Cymru has called for an independent inquiry into the war in Iraq for a number of years. The recent inquiry announced by Gordon Brown on 15 June 2009 is woefully inadequate. Its transparency has been questioned and none of the Inquiry's public meetings will be in Wales – yet again showing the contempt in which Wales is held by the self-serving Westminster elite.

Canada (the country that has suffered the highest number of per capita casualties in Afghanistan) has announced its intention to withdraw its forces from Afghanistan by 2011; another NATO member, the Netherlands, is at the time of writing set to leave next year. The question therefore is whether the US and the UK, the two biggest contributors to the NATO-backed ISAF contingent in Afghanistan, could do the same without harming their strategic interests? Plaid believes that military withdrawal will not damage security in the UK and believes that it is in the interest of people the world over to support the troops and bring them home.

The arguments for withdrawal are relatively uncomplicated. The over-riding rationale for leaving is the cost of staying: in financial terms for the US alone this is estimated to be $60 billion in 2009. It is, of course, the human cost that is weighing most heavily on public and political opinion: at the time of writing, October was the deadliest month yet for the coalition since the US-led invasion in 2001. There is also the human cost for countless innocent people in Afghanistan itself. As in the debate over withdrawal from Iraq, there is some evidence to suggest that the presence of Western military forces is itself part of the problem, allowing the Taliban to justify their armed struggle in religious terms as *jihad*, much as the Mujahideen did when fighting the Soviet-backed Najibullah government in the 1980s.

The principal argument against early withdrawal is that the Taliban will depose the weak and ineffectual Karzai government, reinstating themselves in power in Kabul as in previous years. More time is necessary, it is argued, to develop the capacity of Afghan institutions, especially the Afghan National Army, to become self-sustaining in the face of a continuing insurgent threat. The return of the Taliban, it is feared, would create a 'safe haven' for Al-Qaida, as was the case prior to 9/11, destabilising the wider region, especially Pakistan.

Even if Kabul were to fall to a Taliban-led coalition, it is not clear that this would represent a threat to important Western interests. Pakistan would, in all probability, remain a more attractive base for Al-Qaida's leadership, because its western frontier, though equally remote, is much more impervious to foreign incursion as it forms part of the sovereign territory of a powerful, indeed nuclear-armed state. It also must be borne in mind that the Taliban and Al-Qaida are distinct movements with different political objectives. The Talib Pashtun nationalists are unlikely to welcome the prospect of being ejected from power a second time because of the actions of a few foreign fighters from the Arabian Gulf. Al-Qaida itself has also changed its modus operandi: mass training camps in the deserts of Afghanistan are no longer required, it would appear, as the training for its last two major attacks on Western targets, in the US and the UK respectively, were conducted in a flying school in Florida and an outward bound centre in Wales.

The possibility of a 'domino effect' resulting in a Taliban takeover of Pakistan is also presented as part of the rationale for continuing the war in Afghanistan. This argument is fairly implausible given the much greater strength of the well-established Pakistani Armed Forces vis-à-vis the Pakistani Taliban. A military coup against the current pro-Western government – as has happened before in the history of Pakistan – is a much more likely prospect. Even when considered in this context, there is strong evidence to suggest that it is the presence of Western forces in Afghanistan that is currently the destabilising impetus within Pakistan, not the prospect of their withdrawal.

Why Vote Plaid? Steffan Lewis, Islwyn

'We in 21st-century Wales are presented with a real opportunity: to forge a new Wales – a Wales that will reflect the aspirations of each and every one of our citizens; a vibrant, inclusive, outward-looking Wales. We want to make Wales a better place to live and work. Plaid wants to release our nation's potential and to deliver a better standard of living for all. Plaid is the party for the people of Wales, representing everyone who has chosen to make Wales their home.

My home borough of Islwyn, like all Valleys communities, has its part to play in shaping such a Wales. Our communities, like others across Wales, have been let down by an uncaring Labour Party, once cherished by our people.

Plaid policy priorities for the Valleys include:

- creating safer neighbourhoods and tackling crime, especially alcohol-related crime;
- securing support for individuals and families who are struggling because of the current economic crisis;

- continuing the campaign for a fuel duty regulator, so that duty on fuel decreases as the price of oil rises;
- fighting for a fairer tax system to pay for world-class public services;
- making our area an attractive place to do business by helping local companies thrive;
- finding locally-based ideas to play our part in combating climate change;
- fighting for a better future for our young people, creating opportunities for all.

It's time to make a difference. It's time to make the Valleys matter.'

There is no strategy available to Western governments in Afghanistan that is guaranteed success. What we can say is that a managed withdrawal is less costly than staying indefinitely and its chances of success, in strategic terms, given the inherent uncertainties, is at least comparable. While Plaid advocates a policy of bringing our troops home safely, it must also be the case that for as long as the troops are there, they should be properly equipped and should also be able to look forward to appropriate and enhanced post-conflict care (in the physical, mental and emotional sense) when home.

Defence and international policy

As Plaid's position on both wars in Iraq and Afghanistan should demonstrate, Plaid has a long record as an internationalist party concerned with peace and justice the world over. Plaid believes that inequality and injustice fuel tension and conflict. Creating a fairer world will lead to a safer world. As a contribution to establishing fairer international trade systems, our global trade strategy will include clear steps towards winning international fair trade status for Wales and making Wales an international centre of excellence for socially responsible business and ethical procurement. We will also put forward practical measures for Wales and its people to make a positive contribution to help some of the poorest nations in the world meet the Millennium Development Goals. We will also continue to work for an end to Israeli occupation of Palestinian land as part of a lasting and fair two state solution Plaid will press the British government to stop Britain's involvement in the arms trade on the basis that it causes untold misery and death to millions of people throughout the world, not just by means of their destructive force, but also by diverting resources from socially beneficial activities such as food production, education and health. We will oppose nuclear weapons, in particular the proposed new generation of Trident. Our current positions on international affairs indicate how we'd run a defence policy in future as an independent nation.

- Plaid has consistently and emphatically opposed the Afghanistan and Iraq wars and has called for the immediate withdrawal of UK forces from both countries along with the dismantling of their military bases in Iraq and Afghanistan.
- Plaid supports a peaceful and sustainable two-state solution for Israel and Palestine and an end to the Israeli occupation of Palestinian land.
- Plaid is against nuclear weapons and the proposed new generation of Trident.
- Plaid believes in a strong and robust United Nations.
- Plaid believes that a fairer world is a safer world. Plaid supports fair trade relations, supports an enhanced overseas aid budget, the Millennium Development Goals and is against forcing developing countries to privatise services.

A Plaid government in an independent Wales would:

- seek membership of the European Union and the United Nations;
- always uphold the rule of international law;
- ensure that no nuclear weapons would be based, tested or used in Wales;
- not be part of any nuclear-based commitment such as in NATO;
- not let military training or facilities disrupt communities or ruin rural land, including opposing all low flying exercises;
- guarantee that Welsh soldiers are never again dragged into an illegal war waged against the wishes of Wales. The Welsh Parliament would have the final say on whether service personnel take part in any military conflict.

Existing military infrastructure in Wales would come under Welsh control. A negotiated share of the UK's defence resources would be retained and a small professional force would be organised under a Welsh chain of command answerable to the Welsh Parliament. The role of the military would be decided at the time, depending on the changing threats and security situation, and the aim would be to safeguard our land, sea and air space. Other commitments would be to assist in peacekeeping and civil emergencies in partnership with the world community under the authority of the United Nations. Any defence service would mainly be comprised of infantry with limited air and naval capabilities.

As far as defence expenditure is concerned, it is likely to be much less than our present share through the UK (2.2 per cent GDP or £34.5 billion total) as we would not engage in expensive unilateral campaigns or engage in developing nuclear weapons. Ireland, with a population a million bigger than Wales currently spends 0.7 per cent of its GDP or £700 million on defence and has about 10,000 military personnel. We would look at the Irish model and other international models in deciding the size and cost of our defence policy.

Europe

Plaid is proud of its European heritage and sees Wales at the heart of the European family of nations. Plaid believes in an open and democratic Europe with decisions made as close to the citizen as possible. Wales deserves full membership of the EU like other similar countries, Ireland being an obvious example.

- Plaid wants Wales to be at the heart of Europe as a full member of the EU.
- Plaid recognises the need for reform to tackle the existing democratic deficit.
- Plaid believes that Wales should join the euro at the right time – unfortunately due to Labour's terrible handling of the economy, the UK doesn't currently qualify for membership.
- Plaid supported a referendum on the Lisbon Treaty but thanks to Labour we will not get one.

Labour politicians in Europe consistently fail to stand up for Welsh interests. They failed to deliver the referendum on the Lisbon Treaty which they promised the people. The Tories do everything they can to not talk about Europe. They're divided and are allied to a far-right, racist and homophobic group.

Celebrating our national treasures

Plaid Cymru believes we should celebrate and support the cultural riches of the diverse and vibrant communities that make up modern Wales, and welcome the input of new citizens, without in any way forgetting what makes us a unique nation. Plaid is committed to promoting a confident and creative culture in Wales. Culture and the arts are an integral part of the process of re-generating our communities, creating a sense of identity and developing our potential as a nation.

Plaid led the campaign against the plan to weaken the Arts Council, as we believe that the government should not interfere directly in the arts. The role of government is to create the framework which allows culture to flourish and to give a strategic lead. We welcome the Stephens report into the Arts industry in Wales and will implement many of its recommendations. Plaid believes in promoting artistic and cultural activity for people of all ages and backgrounds in all parts of Wales. Plaid supports the expansion of cultural activity in all the regions of Wales through strategic regional partnerships as part of our vision of creating regional growth centres.

As the model of globalisation means that nations and people come to resemble each other more and more in their cultural compass, so it becomes all the more important to ensure that the Welsh language is helped to thrive and prosper given the historic injustices which Welsh-language speakers have faced over the centuries. The Welsh language is a defining and uniting icon of Welsh culture and identity. More and more parents are choosing to send their children to Welsh-medium education. Plaid believes that the Welsh language belongs to everyone in Wales, whether you speak the language or not. It is a national treasure that Plaid believes should be safeguarded and promoted in order to create a nation which is truly bilingual and where speaking more than one language becomes the norm for the majority of people. As part of the One Wales government, Plaid has prioritised:

- ensuring new Welsh language legislation to confirm official status for both Welsh and English, to establish the post of Language Commissioner and give Welsh language speakers certain rights to use the language;
- creating a national Welsh medium education strategy through developing effective provision from nursery through to further and higher education;
- establishing a Welsh medium higher education network including a federal college as previously described;

- supporting the dot.cym campaign to gain domain name status for Wales on the internet, recognising the importance of ensuring that the Welsh language thrives in on-line communities as well as in geographical ones.

Sport can play a role in making society healthier as well as raising Wales's profile on the international stage. We will make sure that the Sports Council uses its funding to create more sporting opportunities for women and for people with disabilities. We will co-operate with the national bodies responsible for particular sports in Wales to ensure that young people have more opportunities to develop their skills.

We will support and encourage a bid to host the Commonwealth Games in Wales. This would not only raise Wales's international profile but will also be a shop window for the sporting facilities we have in Wales. And we will seek opportunities to ensure that Wales has national teams in as many sports as possible.

Conclusion: Why vote Plaid?

So instead of asking 'why vote Plaid?' perhaps the question should actually be 'why *not* vote Plaid?'. There will always be a plethora of different reasons and motivations for voting Plaid, as summarised in this book.

While it's easy to think that politics is more complicated than it actually is, fundamentally, Plaid has a vision for Wales and is passionate about delivering that vision. That's why Plaid's town, community and county councillors work hard at the grassroots. That's why Plaid AMs, MPs and MEPs do what they do. They're just ordinary people who are doing extraordinary things with the help of people in diverse communities all over Wales.

Plaid will always put the people of Wales first. As a party, Plaid will continue to do what it has done since 1925 in the firm belief that there can be a better Wales. Plaid's aim is to build on our core values to create a party that will be attractive to everyone who has chosen to make Wales their home. Plaid is the only innately Welsh political party in the sense that it does not fight elections anywhere else in the UK and organises politically in Wales alone. Plaid is the only party that is dedicated to listening to the people of Wales and our only loyalty is to the people of Wales. Our defining aim is to cultivate – and ensure – the living and working conditions that will enable the people of Wales to prosper. For Plaid, Wales is a community of communities – a kaleidoscope as opposed to a patchwork quilt with diverse, vibrant and changing communities. It should therefore come as no surprise that devolution to us means more than devolving power to Cardiff alone (as important as it is for us to have a thriving capital city). Devolution means empowering Wales's communities and distributing prosperity to all regions and individuals in Wales and ensuring that decisions are taken at the most appropriate level and as locally as possible.

Plaid wants Wales to play its role in building a more sustainable, peaceful and fair world. As the Copenhagen Climate Change Summit met, combating global warming is the world's most important challenge. As Wales is a land rich in natural resources, Plaid believes that we should make the most of these resources and lead the way, creating innovative solutions as part of our global responsibility to overcoming this crisis. Many nations, much smaller than Wales, are already independent members of the international community. We want equality for Wales so that it too can become an equal partner with the other free nations of the world: its people deserve no less. Plaid is the only party for the people of Wales. We demonstrate this every day in our actions, our policies and in our absolute determination to put the needs of the people of Wales above all else.

Many will vote Plaid because of our ideas and policies which promote fairness, environmental and economic responsibility responding to the triple crunch of peak oil, the climate crisis and the ravages of the recession. These policies emanate from our love for our nation and land, as Plaid wants to cultivate a country and people that aspire towards success and where everyone is given the best possible start in life. Plaid believes that the current political set-up, where power has been exercised over the people of Wales by successive failing London governments, doesn't permit the people of Wales to achieve their full potential. Plaid believes that a proper legislative Parliament in Wales serving the needs of the people of Wales must be our next priority. Until that reality is achieved, and for as long as power lies in Westminster, Plaid MPs will do everything within their power to fight, not only for their constituents, but also for the whole nation ensuring that the Welsh government's political priorities are realised, not hampered, by the UK government.

These are exciting times for Plaid. We have the opportunity now to reach out to all the people of Wales and to engage with them. We mean to embrace the challenges of a new era and grasp the opportunity before us. Its an opportunity to forge a new Wales–a Wales that will reflect the aspirations of each and every one of its citizens. A vibrant, inclusive, outward-looking, prosperous Wales. That is our challenge. That is our motivation.

A–Z of Plaid Cymru

A is for

Adrannau (National Sections) – Women's Section, the Councillors' Section, our youth and student movement Cymru X, Equalities (including Muslims for Plaid), Undeb (our trade union section). These are the party's recognised sections.

B is for

Bilingualism. Plaid Cymru is committed to bilingualism as a basis for multilingualism.

C is for

Cangen. The Cangen (or branch) is the basic building block of party organisation. Every party member belongs to their local branch, which is normally based on a local ward (or collection of wards). Branches have a number of standard office bearers e.g. chair, secretary and treasurer. The more active branches may also have press officers, membership secretaries, youth officers.

Constituency. Branches come together to form constituency committees. There are forty constituency committees, one for each of the National Assembly constituencies in Wales. Every constituency has a chair, a treasurer and a secretary.

D is for

Dafydd. Yes, there are far too many Dafydds in Plaid Cymru. . .

Dd is for

Y Ddraig Goch (the Red Dragon), a quarterly publication by the party, which includes some news about party activity as well as our biannual appeals.

E is for

EFA (European Free Alliance), of which we are a member. We have many sister parties across Europe.

F is for

Finances. Plaid is currently the only party in the UK with no debts.

G is for

Gweithlen. A monthly publication for party officers communicating key pieces of information to constituencies.

H is for

Holidays. Plaid believes that St. David's Day should be a statutory bank holiday.

I is for

Independence.

J is for

Jill Evans. Jill Evans is an MEP and leader of the Plaid Cymru group in the European Parliament.

K is for

Kurds. Plaid has long campaigned against human rights abuses in Kurdistan. Delegates for the KNK visit us at conference on a regular basis.

Ll is for

Llwyd. Elfyn Llwyd MP. The leader of our group in Westminster.

M is for

Membership. We serve our members. Without them, we would simply not be here.

N is for

National Register of Candidates. A member must be on the register in order to be considered to stand for Assembly, Westminster, European elections, etc.

O is for

Offices. We have several all over Wales (for AMs/MPs/MEPs/ constituency offices).

P is for

Post-Its. Plaid Post-Its. The name for our e-bulletin that goes usually once a week to members and supporters.

R is for

Regional co-ordinators. They sit on the National Executive Committee and represent different geographical regions from within the party.

T is for

Target seats. Those constituencies where we focus and target our resources to win in a given election.

U is for

There is no U. Well, there is actually. Uned Datblygu, our new Development Unit (launched in August 2009).

W is for

Wales.

X is for

Plaid Cymru, or at least we hope that all voters will put their X next to Plaid Cymru.

Z is for

Zeitgeist.

To join Plaid or to find out more, get in touch:

Address
Plaid Cymru
Tŷ Gwynfor
Marine Chambers
Anson Court
Atlantic Wharf
Cardiff
CF10 4AL

Phone
029 2047 2272

E-mail
post@plaidcymru.org

Web
www.plaidcymru.org
www.plaidlive.com
www.youtube.com/plaidtv

Twitter
twitter.com/plaid_cymru

Facebook
Plaid Cymru

SUSAN OWEN AND ANGELA HAINE

Discovering
Walks in Surrey

SHIRE PUBLICATIONS LTD

Contents

The maps were drawn by Richard G. Holmes. The cover photograph of Shere is by Cadbury Lamb.

Copyright © 1981 by Susan Owen and Angela Haine. First published 1981. Number 264 in the Discovering series. ISBN 0 85263 560 5.

Set in 9 on 9 point English Times by Permanent Typesetting & Printing Co Ltd, Hong Kong, and printed in Great Britain by C. I. Thomas & Sons (Haverfordwest) Ltd, Press Buildings, Merlins Bridge, Haverfordwest.

Introduction

This book of walks in Surrey has been produced as the result of our walking together as friends, about once or twice a month, over the past fifteen or so years. We have greatly enjoyed devising and compiling these walks (all of which are circular and of widely varying lengths) and hope that they will give pleasure to those who follow in our footsteps.

We have tried to include walks in most parts of Surrey, although, inevitably in a book of this length, there are some large areas of countryside in which we have not managed to include a walk. The scenery changes dramatically with the changing seasons and maybe you will find that a viewpoint or particular aspect we have mentioned is not visible in high summer because of dense foliage. We hope that the walks will be easy to follow and that, if some features of the countryside have altered since the walks were written (e.g. paths rerouted for various reasons or stiles and gates replaced), the sketch maps provided and the relevant Ordnance Survey maps (186 or 187) will be found helpful in keeping to the general direction of the walk.

One important change which will affect two of the walks (numbers 8 and 12) is the new M25 motorway, which is expected to be completed by 1985. We have, however, obtained the large-scale plans of the affected footpaths and have given details of bridges over and under the motorway, so that the walks will be only slightly rerouted.

As regards footwear, some attempt has been made to indicate the amount of mud to be encountered, but we have found that boots or wellingtons are best for winter walking when the bridleways and farm paths can become churned up by horses and cattle; even in the summer, after prolonged rain, some paths can be impassable with ordinary shoes.

We should like to acknowledge the help we have received from our families and friends in preparing and checking these walks and, in particular, we wish to thank Peggy Chester, Pam and Peter Wallis, Beryl Jennings and Mary Garvie, amongst others, for their assistance and encouragement. We are also indebted to the Warden of Holmbury St Mary youth hostel, Howard Piner, and his brother Geoff for suggesting Walk 9, which starts from outside the youth hostel.

We hope that you will enjoy your rambles in this beautiful county.

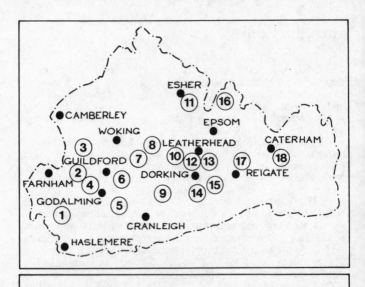

KEY TO SKETCH MAPS

✳	START OF WALK
◄━━···	ROUTE OF WALK
Ⓟ	CAR PARK
═══	ROAD
=====	TRACK
----	OTHER FOOTPATHS
■	BUILDING
✝	CHURCH
P.O.	POST OFFICE
P.H.	PUBLIC HOUSE
～～～	RIVER OR STREAM
◌	WATER FEATURE
+●+	RAILWAY AND STATION
)(	BRIDGE

1. Frensham Little Pond, the Devil's Jumps and Yagden Hill

Distance: 7 or 6 miles.
Grid reference: 859418.
Ordnance Survey maps: 1:50,000 sheet 186; 1:25,000 sheets SU84 and SU83

A lovely walk on the extensive sandy heathlands bordering Frensham Little Pond and the Devil's Jumps, where there are magnificent views across to the Hog's Back and to Hampshire and Sussex. The walk continues over Kettlebury and Yagden Hills to Stockbridge Pond and Tilford. There are no stiles and very little mud and the stiffish climb up the Devil's Jump can be avoided if wished.

Bus: The 217 Alder Valley (Farnham-Grayshott, not Sundays) stops outside the post office in Rushmoor village. Cross the road from the garage to the bridleway opposite by the MOD sign and continue the walk at the paragraph marked (*).
Car park: There is a large car park at Frensham Little Pond situated on a minor road near the lake about a mile from the A287. From Hindhead take the first turning on the right after Frensham Great Pond.
Refreshments: There are inns at Tilford and Churt and a post office and general store in Rushmoor.

From the large car park at Frensham Little Pond, cross the grassy playing area to the road opposite the toilets and skirt the top of the lake. Just by a much smaller parking area, turn half-right on a path by a National Trust sign and go through wooden barriers by the side of the lake, soon crossing over a stream in a hollow by some sluice gates. Keeping the lake on the right, continue along its banks for a few hundred yards and, where the path forks by some concrete posts at the corner of a field, still keep on the narrow path by the lake. On coming to the end of this part of the lake, continue on a path between wire fences with a field on the left. After nearly half a mile, pass through a metal barrier by a field where horses are kept, continue over a crossing track and almost immediately turn right down a dirt track just before a house.

At a minor road turn left for about 100 yards and by a house on the left cross the road to a bridleway opposite. Follow the path across the heathland towards the three peaks of the Devil's Jumps, soon coming to a beautiful secluded lake, fringed with rhododendrons and pines. Branch off on a path with the lake on the right, towards a pine grove, and continue round to the end of the lake. Fork left and, on reaching the main path once more, turn right to a junction of paths. Continue forward on a wide sandy path towards the highest of the three peaks. At a crossing track, one can avoid climbing the hill by turning left on a path, with two houses slightly to the right on the skyline, and cross the heath to join the walk shortly before the post office in Rushmoor. For the more energetic it is well worth the short steep climb for the magnificent views from the top towards the Hog's Back to the north and across to Hindhead to the south. Go over the crossing track and bear slightly left, soon climbing up the steep side of the hill.

If you wish to visit the Pride of the Valley inn at Churt, cross the reddish stone crag at the summit and go down a path the other side which soon reaches a wire fence, turn left and at the corner of the fence turn right down to the road. Turn left for the inn and rejoin the walk by turning left at the road for about half a mile to the post office at Rushmoor. To avoid the road walking, turn left at the crag on the summit and take the sandy path down some wooden steps. At a fork keep right for a few yards and go to the right of some bushes in the centre of a small clearing. Bear right to take a path on the right. At a wire fence turn left and follow the fence down past some houses until you come to a wide sandy track. Turn right between fences out to the road. Turn left over Sandy Lane to the post office and bus stop at Rushmoor.

(*)Cross the road from the garage to a path by a Ministry of Defence notice leading into Hankley Common. Soon go over a small stream up to a large clearing with telegraph wires. Cross the clearing to take the wide path uphill. Continue on this path, ignoring paths off to either side, until you come to some tall pines. Take the wide sandy path on the left of the trees and follow it uphill and then cross the shallow valley to the hill beyond. Bear right to the top of Kettlebury Hill and turn left on a broad track with fine views to the right. At a fork just past a pillbox, keep right. After nearly a mile on this fine ridge path, at a meeting of paths called the Lion's Mouth and just before a wire fence on the right, bear left downhill towards a wooden barrier on a hill ahead. At the bottom of the slope, cross over a track and continue between wire fences, bearing off to the left towards the golf course. On coming to a wooden hut by the eleventh tee, turn right along a path by Yagden Hill. When this path divides into three, take the left-hand path going slightly downhill. Go over a crossing track and at a T junction turn left. At a wide clearing in the woods, take the path on the left and follow this down to a small car park near Stockbridge Pond. Go along the unmade track with the pond on the left until you reach the road.

At this point one can take a short cut back to the car park at

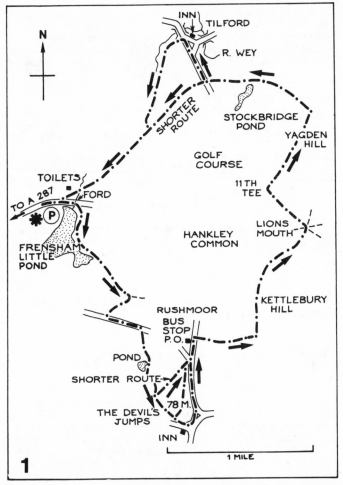

Frensham Little Pond or extend the walk slightly by visiting Tilford and returning via the river Wey.

For the shorter route, cross the road to a bridleway opposite and follow the path for about a mile and a half, keeping left at a fork, eventually passing the toilets to reach the road by the car park.

For the longer route, turn right along the road for about a quarter of a mile towards the green at Tilford. This large triangle of turf is famous for its cricket pitch and the ancient oak on the north side of the green, which is reckoned to be some nine hundred years old and is 10 feet (3.05 m) in diameter at its widest point. The Barley Mow inn was built in about 1700. The shallow water at the foot of the picturesque bridge is much favoured by canoeists and paddlers in the summer months. At the end of the cricket green, just before another bridge ahead, turn left to a public footpath through a small gate. After passing the delightful Malt House, keep forward on a small path and at a crossing path turn right on a grassy path which leads down to the river Wey. Continue on the track between wire fences and go through a gate to enter a wood. Go over a crossing track and continue forward to join a track coming in from the left. At the end of some outbuildings, go forward on a path through the trees. This path eventually joins another track. Turn right and continue along the track for about half a mile to go over a water splash and past the toilets for the car park.

To return to the bus stop at Rushmoor, turn left on reaching the road, passing the end of the lake to continue the walk by taking the path by the National Trust sign mentioned in the first paragraph.

2. Puttenham Common, Waverley Abbey and Tilford

Distance: 11, 7½ or 4½ miles.
Grid references: 919461 (walks A and C); 910457 (walk B).
Ordnance Survey maps: 1:50,000 sheet 186; 1:25,000 sheets SU94 and SU84.

This walk of 11 miles can be split into two parts. Walk A from the upper car park at Puttenham Common is 4½ miles and crosses the common to the lakes and then returns via Cut Mill Pond and field paths to the car park. Walk B (7½ miles) starts from the lower car park near The Tarn and goes over Crooksbury Common to pass the ruins of Waverley Abbey on the far banks of the river Wey. It then passes through Tilford and returns to the car park by pleasant paths and bridleways. Walk C combines both walks.

Bus: The Alder Valley bus from Puttenham stops outside the upper car park at Puttenham Common and also the lower car park at the crossroads at Cut Mill.
Car parks: Walks A and C start from the large car park at

Puttenham Common. At the post office in Puttenham village, turn left down Suffield Lane, signposted to Elstead and Cut Mill. After about 1½ miles turn right into the car park. The entrance is rather concealed and is on a fairly sharp right-hand bend. Walk B starts from the car park near the crossroads at Cut Mill about a mile further on. Turn right to the car park.

Refreshments: In Tilford, or the Donkey inn at Charleshill, in Walks B and C.

For Walks A and C

At the large car park at Puttenham Common, where there are fine views across to Crooksbury Hill and the wireless mast which is passed in Walks B and C, make for a prominent Surrey Open Space sign to the right of some sandy hillocks. Take the path at the foot of the hillocks and go down a steep slope into a shallow valley and straight up the path on the other side. In a wooded glade, keep on in the same direction uphill, ignoring crossing tracks. Take the right fork in the wood, passing a path coming downhill from the right, and continue slightly left downhill and up the other side of a valley to a T junction. Turn right uphill on a sandy path to reach a wide sandy track. Turn left along this broad track for about half a mile to some woods by a fence. Turn left downhill, passing the large Hampton Park estate on the right, and soon the rather muddy General's Pond on the left. Keep on the path to the large lakes called Warren Pond and The Tarn.

On reaching the causeway between the two lakes cross this and follow the path round the lake on the left, over the small footbridge. Where the path leaves the lake, follow it through the trees to a small car park near the road. Turn right for about 500 yards and at a bend, opposite a house on the right, cross the road to a divergence of paths. Walks A and C divide at this point.

For Walk A, take the cart track going slightly uphill with telegraph poles on the left, and follow this track past a new pumping station on the right for over half a mile to reach a minor road. Turn left for a few hundred yards to a definite crossing track. Turn right to cross the common out to a road. Bear slightly left and cross the road to the bridleway opposite to join Walk C again at the last paragraph.

For Walk B. At the car park, on the right of the crossroads coming from Puttenham and bordering the lake, continue up the road for about 500 yards to a bend, opposite a house on the right.

For Walks B and C. At the divergence of paths opposite the house, take the sandy track on the right between gateposts. After about a quarter of a mile, where the path divides, take the centre path going on in the same direction with a pinewood on the left. Keep on this path, ignoring side turnings, and at a wood, where the path bends to the right, keep on the main sandy path through the centre of the wood. On reaching the road, turn right and in about a quarter of a mile turn left at a bridlepath sign. This small path soon joins a wide track. Keep ahead under telegraph wires at a turning to the left, and at the next turning bend left slightly uphill. At a fork of sandy tracks, keep right and continue on this track for about half a mile to a T junction by a notice saying 'Crooksbury Conservation Area'. Turn right and after some way, after passing a house on the right and two houses on the left, turn off left on a wide path. On coming to a minor road ahead, turn left, soon passing the very tall wireless mast which was seen from Puttenham Common car park.

Turn right for a short distance at the road, and then turn left down a small unmade-up road, with names of some cottages on a tree. After passing the delightful Crooksbury Cottage, this track leads down to a road where you turn right. In about 300 yards, at a right-hand bend, turn left down a sandy track, which soon becomes rather muddy. The river Wey is just visible through the trees down on the right. When the track becomes sandy again, turn off right towards some posts on a pretty path through a rhododendron wood, soon with a vista across the water meadows to the ruins of Waverley Abbey. This Cistercian house was founded as early as 1128 and was the first Cistercian monastery in England. It was damaged by a serious flooding of the Wey in 1233. After leaving the river and climbing up a small hill, the path divides and we take the left-hand fork. Keep on this path with fields on one side and a wood on the other and ignore a left turning after some way. On joining a cart track, just past a notice saying 'Herons Wey Surrey West Girl Guides', with the Wey ahead, turn left along the track. Go through a gate to reach a road and turn right towards a picturesque river bridge. Almost immediately turn left up a path going uphill. After passing the beautiful Tilhill House on the left, branch off to the right, with the river down on the right. On reaching the road it is worth turning right over the much photographed bridge at Tilford to the beautiful cricket green and the Barley Mow Inn.

To continue the walk, retrace your steps over the bridge and go past the Post Office and Stores. After a few hundred yards, just before a sharp bend to the left, take the first small road to the right and turn left by a grassy triangle to go immediately right on a drive. At the end of the drive, take the footpath on the right. This is a beautiful path with fine views to the right looking across to Hankley Common and beyond. Cross over two minor roads and then cross a track to continue on the same footpath out to a road. Turn right and continue along the road until just past the Donkey inn on the right.

Cross the road and go up a track for a short way, then turn right up a sandy path. This soon joins a metalled drive by the

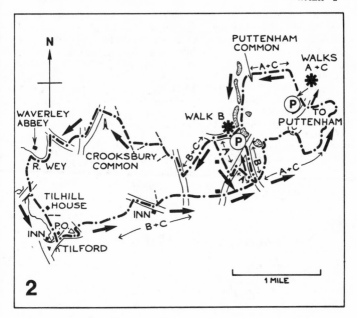

2

1 MILE

entrance to a large estate. On reaching some tall wrought iron gates, turn left and continue down the drive past the stone entrance pillars out to the road. Cross this to the bridleway opposite, which eventually leads out past Fulbrook Farm to a road. Cross the road to the cart track opposite, and after about 150 yards go through a small gate in the fence bordering a field, opposite a white post. Cross the field diagonally right to a just visible gate. Go through the gate and continue down a small path, cross over a reddish stream and soon come out to a road. (For Walk B turn left and continue on this road to the car park by the crossroads.) Turn left and after a short distance, after a cottage on the right, pass a minor road and then immediately take the bridleway into the woods on the right.

For Walks A and C. Keep on this bridleway until reaching a brick track. Cross this towards Cutmill Pond and go over a small bridge with railings. Follow the path round by the edge of the attractive pond. Keep on past a flight of wooden steps down on the right to join the drive at the end of a grassy bank. Turn right and follow the drive with a hedge on the left and an old wall on the right. When the drive ends by a house, take the path ahead between the wall and a garage, first crossing over some wooden planks. After a short distance, this path can become rather overgrown with nettles and it is possible to cut up to the field on the left and continue close to the hedge to follow the path out on to a lane. Turn right along this for a short way, and where the drive goes into a house, bear off slightly right to a public bridleway sign. At the next T junction turn left and continue on a wide and sandy track. At a junction turn left and after some way go under telegraph wires by a bend and take the main path bearing left into a wood. When the path comes out at a field, turn left and keep along the edge of the field to a path in the wood. Continue round a bend with wide views to the left, and at the next bend bear right into a wood and *immediately* left on to a rather indistinct path through the wood. At a T junction by a public footpath sign turn left and then right uphill on a very small path to a cottage and a road. Cross the road to the car park and bus stop at Puttenham Common.

3. Normandy, Ash and Flexford

Distance: 6½ miles.
Grid reference: 927516.
Ordnance Survey maps: 1:50,000 sheet 186; 1:25,000 sheets SU95 and SU94.

This walk of about 6½ miles first crosses Normandy Common, then ventures on the wild heathland and pinewoods skirting the army ranges. After climbing Normandy Hill, with excellent views across the ranges and towards the Hog's Back, we descend towards Ash and continue on a very different terrain following farm lanes and footpaths across fields. This latter part of the walk can be muddy and boots are advisable.

Trains: From Ash station, join the walk by turning left and almost immediately right over a small footbridge by a 'No horses' sign. Cross a field planted with vegetables and at a minor road turn right to join the walk at (*).
Buses: Alder Valley, Guildford to Aldershot, stops in Normandy village near the Spar food store. The car park is opposite.
Cars: Car park opposite Spar food store on A323 at minor cross-roads, just past Normandy village, if coming from Guildford.
Refreshments: Inns in Normandy and Ash.

Cross the footbridge on the left at the rear of the car park, pass some swings and follow the path through the woods, over another bridge and on towards Normandy football ground. Turn left at

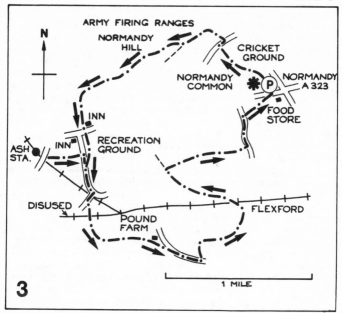

3

1 MILE

the football pitch towards a cottage and after passing this the path soon comes to a footbridge at a junction of paths. Take the path between holly bushes directly opposite the bridge, i.e. turn right, going slightly uphill on a pleasant path, which eventually emerges at a well kept cricket ground. Turn left and skirt the ground, going past some wooden posts near the pavilion. Turn left immediately, cross a stile and follow the path towards a road, forking left about 100 yards before the road is reached. Cross a stile out on to the road and turn right for about 50 yards before crossing over to a track just after some houses, marked by a notice warning you not to touch suspicious objects.

After a short distance, turn right by a Ministry of Defence notice near a barred entrance. Follow the track to open heathland where the flagpoles denoting the danger areas are situated. If the red flags are flying the rattle of the guns should be evident by now. Do not venture near the flags but bear left here with pines on the left. Ignore a side turning on the left after a short distance and continue on this broad track, which soon descends into a shallow depression. There is a path of sorts on the right here in the woods if the track is waterlogged. Keep on past a wide right-hand turning and then a crossing track and at the next crossing track turn right towards Normandy Hill. Follow this narrow sandy path and at a junction keep forward on a stony track going steeply up to the top of the hill. There are marvellous views here across to the Hog's Back and over the firing ranges.

At the top of the hill, cross the clearing slightly left and continue forward on a stony path which bears round to the right, soon to reach another clearing. Cross this, keeping to the edge of the slope, to take a path half-right going downhill between pines. This beautiful path eventually comes to a small fork; bear left and at a crossing track almost immediately keep forward on a track going downhill. On reaching a solitary Scots pine, bear right across a large clearing with a shallow pond in the centre and keep slightly right over some hillocks with a wire fence on the left. At the corner of the wire fence, turn left past some houses down to a car park and out to a road. Cross this slightly right to an opening opposite. There are inns on both sides of the road here. Cross the recreation ground and out through a metal gate on the right to a small road by some cottages. Turn to the left.

(*)Keep on this minor road for about a quarter of a mile and when the road bends sharply left go right over the railway bridge, signposted Hog's Back, and past a pheasantry and other wildfowl on the right. Soon turn left at a public footpath sign opposite a cottage. The path can be muddy but soon improves and becomes a cinder track. At a road turn left over a bridge across a disused railway track. Just past a shed on the right turn off left through woods on a rather wet path, but drier alternatives can be found. At a line of bungalows turn left down a wide green avenue lined with trees.

After passing Pound Farm and a duckpond turn right on to a metalled road. Continue past some houses and a farm until the road degenerates into a cart track. After about 100 yards turn left down a footpath. After some way this path bends sharply right and continues downhill through woods, eventually coming to a metalled lane leading past some bungalows on the outskirts of Flexford. Just before a railway embankment, turn left by a footpath sign and follow the path between wire fences, crossing two stiles and then over the railway line. Go down through a copse and over a very tall stile out to a field. Cross the field diagonally right, over a drainage ditch in the centre and on to a path leading to a gap in the hedges between two fields. Cross the next field with a lane on the right and at the end of the field go over a wooden plank and up some steps and continue along the edge of the third field to a stile out on to the lane on the right. After passing under some pylons turn right at the end of the wood along a cart track. A pond can be seen away to the left here. Follow the main path, ignoring side turnings, and on coming to an open field keep to the left-hand edge of the field with a line of pylons on the right.

Cross the stile at the end of the field and continue on a path with a wire fence on the left through a narrow belt of trees. Go through a gate at the end of the field and continue ahead to another gate with a copse on the right. Keep on in the same direction past some buildings out to a road. Turn left and walk along the road for about a quarter of a mile. At the end of some cottages on the left turn right down a footpath. Go through a gate or over a rickety stile and follow the clear path diagonally left across a field to reach the main road after passing the backs of some houses. Turn right to the car park. (For Ash station, continue from the first paragraph.)

4. Compton, Puttenham and Shackleford

Distance: 7½ miles.
Grid reference: 956471.
Ordnance Survey maps: 1:50,000 sheet 186; 1:25,000 sheet SU94.

This walk encompasses the attractive villages of Compton, Puttenham and Shackleford and is chiefly along field paths and the Pilgrims' Way. The tenth-century church at Compton with its unique two-storeyed chancel is well worth a visit and we go near the Watts Gallery, which contains a large number of the artist's paintings. There is not too much mud and no steep hills.

Buses: The Alder Valley bus 265 or 266, Guildford-Farnham, stops outside the church in Compton village.
Car park: From the Godalming bypass (A3) turn down to Compton. There is a large car park on the left almost opposite the church. The entrance to the car park is down the side of the craft shop.
Refreshments: Inns and general stores in each of the three villages.

From the craft shop turn left through Compton and take the third turning on the left, Polsted Lane, which is on the far side of an open space used as playing fields. After about a quarter of a mile, just before a 'No through road' sign, take the footpath on the left through a wooden gate. After nearly half a mile cross a two-barred fence and make for a stile in the right-hand corner of the field. Continue along this path between fences to a stile ahead and turn left. The tall building in red brick, looking rather like a Greek Orthodox chapel, standing on a hillock on the left is a memorial chapel to the artist G. F. Watts and was erected by the artist's wife in 1896. There is a water tower on the skyline on the left which is seen later in the walk from the opposite direction.

Just before some farm sheds turn right into woods and immediately left on a path through the trees which runs parallel to the farm. Cross a stile to reach a minor road. The Watts Gallery is on the right a short distance down the road and the times of opening can be seen outside. Cross the road to a wide cart track opposite, marked North Downs Way, and continue under the bridge carrying the Godalming bypass. Take the middle track with the camping sign and continue along the Pilgrims' Way, passing clearings in the woods for tents. At a junction follow the North Downs Way sign once more, passing the beautiful Puttenham Heath golf course on the left. This path eventually merges with a small metalled road which leads out to Hook Lane opposite the Jolly Farmer inn.

Keep on the North Downs Way by turning right and then left towards Puttenham. This is an attractive village with many beautiful old houses and cottages. After passing the church, turn left down Suffield Lane and at the end of the wall continue forward following the footpath sign across some pleasantly undulating fields, keeping a wire fence on the left. At the end of the field there is a fine view looking back towards the church, priory and Hog's Back, an ancient trackway of pre-Roman times. Ignore the gate to a field and take the stile ahead by a hedge, continue over two more stiles and follow the straight path ahead by a wire fence. Here you will see the water tower again on the left. At the end of the fence go round the edge of a field to a 'squeeze' in the fence and go straight across the next field to a copse and continue down a dip to a three-barred fence ahead. Follow the fence past a water trough, round to the right and over a stile on to a road.

Turn left and carry on up the road to an old barn standing in some fields on the right. Turn right on to a public footpath, passing the barn on the left. Continue on this path between fields out on to a lane. Turn right and, at the T junction in the picturesque little village of Shackleford, turn left through the village, past a turning to Cut Mill on the right, to a fork by a post office. Bear left up Grenville Road for a short distance and then leave the road in favour of Rokers Lane on the left. After about half a mile you come to a main road. Cross this to take the track ahead with storage sheds on the right. Follow the path through the large market garden to a road and continue in the same direction up the road ahead. Turn left on a marked footpath by a telephone pole. At the end of this short path, cross the road and take the small residential road opposite. At a fork go down a narrow downhill path on the right of a gatepost to a house.

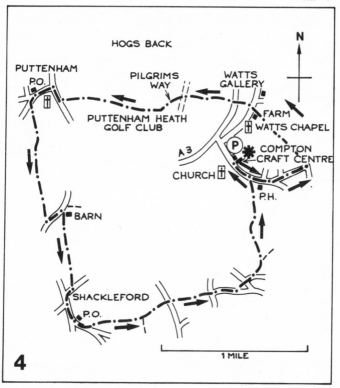

At the field at the bottom of the path turn left through the swing gate and follow the path between fences and hedges out to a cart track. Continue uphill and just before the white manor house on the right, climb over a stile on the left by a stunted tree and cross the field diagonally right to the edge of a copse. Go over a two-barred fence and continue on with a fence on the left. Cross two further stiles past the farmyard and go down a narrow path between fences, over a concrete stile and out to the road by the side of the Harrow public house. Turn left towards the church and car park, passing on the left a sixteenth-century building, White House, formerly the White Hart inn.

5. Winkworth Arboretum, Hydons Ball and Hascombe

Distance: 9, 7 or 6 miles.
Grid references: 989412 (main car park), 997415 (lower car park).
Ordnance Survey maps: 1:50,000 sheet 186; 1:25,000 sheets SU94, SU93 and TQ03.

This is a lovely walk starting from Winkworth Arboretum near Godalming, with its fine displays of azaleas and rhododendrons in spring and glorious autumnal colouring. From the arboretum the walk crosses Juniper Valley and Hydons Heath to climb Hydons Ball and then over Hydons Heath to Hascombe village. The longer walk encircles Hascombe Hill with its iron age encampment and fine views across the Weald to the South Downs.

Bus: 260, Farncombe-Dunsfold, stops outside Winkworth Arboretum – infrequent service.
Car: There are two car parks in the arboretum – the lower car park is reached from Guildford by turning right in Bramley village off the A281 on a minor road for about 2 miles. This gives the opportunity of walking through the arboretum and adds about half a mile to the walk in both directions. The main car park is off the B1230, about 2 miles south of Godalming.
Refreshments: There is a National Trust refreshment chalet in the arboretum, open from May to September from 2 to 6 pm, except Mondays and Fridays, and at weekends in March and April, weather permitting. There is also an inn in Hascombe village.

From the lower car park at the arboretum, go through the gate by the sign that gives times of opening for refreshments. At another gate just before the lake turn right on a path bordering the end of the lake and go up the steps between the azaleas. Turn right at a crossing track and continue on past the toilets and refreshment hut to the main car park.

From the main car park, keep to the left of the parking area and go through a gap in the fence to cross the road to a lane opposite, marked 'South Munstead Lane and Farm'. When the lane bends to the right, bear left by a South Munstead farm sign. At the driveway to a cottage ahead, go down a narrow stony path, ignoring side paths marked 'Private'. Continue on through pinewoods and down to a T junction. Turn left and after a few yards go through a small gate and immediately take the right-hand path going uphill with a field down to the left. Bear right at a T junction and, on emerging at a lane, cross to a path opposite

18

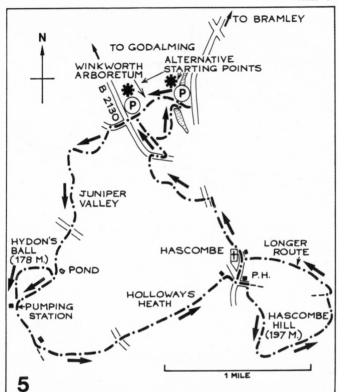

and keep on ahead over two crossing tracks. Shortly after the second crossing path, keep left on the narrower path and at a meeting of tracks almost at once continue forward and keep to the right fork by a pond ahead. On reaching a junction of paths by an enormous beech tree on the left, you have the choice either to climb Hydons Ball or to take a short cut round the bottom of the hill.

To climb Hydons Ball, turn right just before the beech tree and in about 20 yards turn right at a crossing track. (If you do not wish to climb the hill, turn left at the crossing track and continue down to a pumping station ahead – the walk over the hill descends to this point.) Almost immediately turn left under a bar and then take the right fork uphill, ignoring small crossing tracks. This path leads up to the Hydons Ball trig point with its underground water tanks marked by manhole covers. The view is somewhat marred by the pines that have been planted too close to the top but there are glimpses of the magnificent panorama of the South Downs. There is also a seat dedicated to Octavia Hill, one of the founders of the National Trust. Keep across the clearing in the same direction, passing close by the manhole cover beyond the trig point, and take the path ahead leading downhill. Ignore a left turn and at a T junction with a fence ahead turn left downhill passing a memorial stone on the right. At the bottom of the hill continue forward with the pumping station on the right.

For those who did not climb the hill, turn left at the pumping station. Continue along this track and after passing a bungalow on the left turn left on to a narrow public bridleway which climbs up above the track. Keep on this pretty path, which weaves through the trees with an occasional glimpse of lovely views on the right. Shortly after leaving the edge of a field, at a fork where the path goes downhill, bear left. At the entrance to a field, go through a gate and keep on in the same direction with a barbed-wire fence on the right. Chinthurst tower can be seen in the distance on the left. Go through the gate into the next field and enter the wood at a gate. Wild deer can sometimes be seen here. At the minor road cross to a path opposite and continue forward when a path comes in on the right. Keep on this path across Holloways Heath through a beautiful larchwood and then into a silver birch copse.

The path, after about a mile, leads down into the valley past an old house on the left. At a pond bear right and go through a gate to cross a field to the inn ahead at Hascombe village.

For the longer walk (9 miles), at the White Horse inn go up the drive to the right of the inn, turn right by a house and go to the right of a wooden garage to take a sunken footpath. At a junction of paths bear left and continue uphill when another track comes in on the right. When the path divides (open views on the left) take the right-hand track leading into a wood with rhododendrons. On coming to a clearing with some huge beech trees the path should be to the right, but this was blocked by fallen trees and the path can be regained by crossing the track to go up a small slope, then bending to the right on a small path through the trees, which soon rejoins the main path running along the escarpment of Hascombe Hill, with tremendous views across to the Sussex Downs when not obstructed by the trees in leaf. When the track forks ahead, take the left fork going slightly uphill. Later there is a fine rural view to the left looking down the valley to the hills in the distance. At the bottom of the hill, by a gate into a field, turn right up a sunken track. After a short way, turn left through an avenue of trees with a field to the left. On coming to a fork by some cypress trees, go left between wooden gateposts. Continue on this broad sandy track, ignoring side turnings, for about three quarters of a mile. Later the path leads behind some houses to join a lane by a picturesque pond with Hascombe church ahead. Bear right past the noisy geese and hens.

If you do not wish to go round Hascombe Hill, turn down the 'no through road' to the left of the inn, go past the village pond and bear left past the geese and hens.

Both walks continue together. Just before a house facing you on the left, turn off the metalled road to a path on the left and at a fork keep on the path past a wooden barrier on the left. On reaching a stony track continue forward past some stables and go through a gate and on to another metal gate ahead. Turn left on a path between fields to cross a road to a small drive opposite by a house. At the end of the drive, keep on up the hill on a deeply indented path. After passing a fine manor house at the top turn left by a brick wall on to a metalled road. Turn right at the junction up to the main road. Turn right along the road towards two houses on the left. Take the small path between the houses over a stile and continue along this enclosed path. If the lower car park is required, turn right at the first turning. For refreshments, main car park and bus stop continue on this path.

6. Chilworth, Shalford and the Chantries

Distance: 5½ miles (7 miles from Chilworth station).
Grid reference: 024476.
Ordnance Survey maps: 1:50,000 sheet 186; 1:25,000 sheets TQ04 and SU94.

A very varied walk through farmland to Shalford and on to the water meadows and towpath of the river Wey leading to Guildford. The return journey is made along the Chantries with fine views across to Hascombe Hill. Very little mud will be encountered.

Trains: Chilworth and Albury station. Turn left from the station along the A248, Dorking Road, and take the first turning on the right, Blacksmith Lane.
Buses: 425, 439, 450 (Monday-Saturday). Bus stop in A248 by Blacksmith Lane.
Car park: Turn right (if coming from Albury) after passing Chilworth station down Blacksmith Lane. Either park in this lane or turn sharp right at the end into Halfpenny Lane and park on

the verge of the road on the right.
Refreshments: Inns at Shalford and Guildford.

At the sharp bend to the right where Blacksmith Lane joins Halfpenny Lane, take the signposted footpath across the road which goes uphill between fences. After a short time you will see Chilworth Manor on the right through the trees. This house has origins going back to Saxon times and was once owned by Sarah, widow of the great Duke of Marlborough. When the path emerges on to Halfpenny Lane once more, turn left and almost immediately take the path across the fields by the letter box. After nearly a mile the track reaches a farm; climb the stile in the hedge on the right and bear left, i.e. continue in a forward direction. There is a fine view of the ruins of St Catherine's Priory on a little knoll ahead, on the other side of the Wey, which is passed later in the walk. After a short time you can see Guildford Cathedral on the right.

At a small residential road turn left and immediately left again on to a small footpath running parallel to the road. Cross a road to some steps opposite and a stile and continue forward alongside a barbed-wire fence through a field of horses, over the Tilling-bourne to the fine eighteenth-century watermill at Shalford. This was a working corn mill until 1914 and is sometimes open to the public. Keep forward past the mill out on to the main road with the Sea Horse public house opposite. This is the village of Shalford and the church is a short distance along the road to the right. This was rebuilt in 1846 and the pulpit is carved with ships and a shield as a memorial to a young sailor who was lost with his ship in the First World War. By the church is Shalford House, dating back to Tudor times though externally late eighteenth-century; it belonged to the Austen family for three hundred years.

Turn right from the mill and cross the road to a footpath by the side of the Sea Horse car park. When this track bends to the left carry on for a few yards to a five-barred gate and turn left alongside a wire fence with views over the water meadows. When this path ends, cross the stile on the right and go downhill to the river Wey. Follow the path, keeping the river on the right, and cross a small footbridge at the weir, past a cottage on the right (see the flood mark on the gate) and continue along the towpath to the lock. Cross two bridges to the far towpath and follow the path along to Guildford. This is a very pleasant path with plenty of interest along the route. In the summer pleasure boats take visitors from Guildford to Godalming and at the landing stage for the ferry there is a small grotto on the left marking the site where the pilgrims crossed the river. If you wish to visit the ruins of St Catherine's Priory continue up the small road by the grotto and you will see the ruins at the top of the hill on the left.

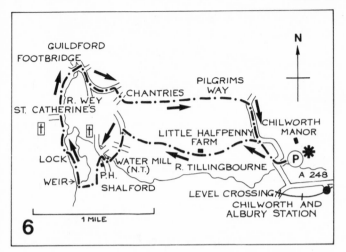

1 MILE

At the end of the towpath cross the footbridge on to the main road. Guildford town is away to the left as is the Yvonne Arnaud Theatre, which was built by public subscription and opened in 1965. To continue the walk turn right and then second left up Chantry View Road. Just before number 38, Gatesgarth, turn right through white posts down a small passage to a road. Cross to the lane opposite, marked North Downs Way, and at the white cottage at the end of the lane take the entrance to the right marked 'Guildford Nature Trail'. The path leads steeply uphill through the Chantries for about half a mile. At the top, where there is a large clearing with some seats, keep ahead on the same path. By a red pole marked '7', bear right along the path, eventually coming to a stile. Cross the stile and turn left, keeping to the edge of the wood, and continue along the open downs with marvellous views across to Hascombe Hill and beyond on the right. Pass through a gap in the hedge and go forward through a gap in the trees in the same direction. Here one can see the small church of St Martha's ahead in its commanding position on top of the hill.

At the end of the open downs go over a two-barred fence on the left and take the path steeply downhill on the right. Turn right at the T junction at the bottom of the hill out on to the lane. Turn right again and on the corner by the 'No horses' sign go down the path on the right between hedges. This leads back to the corner by Halfpenny Lane where the walk started. For the station and buses continue on down Blacksmith Lane for the main road.

7. Ripley, the Wey Navigation and Pyrford

Distance: 6½ or 4 miles.
Grid reference: 053569.
Ordnance Survey maps: 1:50,000 sheets 187 and 188; 1:25,000 sheet TQ05.

A walk along the banks of the Wey Navigation canal and the river Wey with diversions to the twelfth-century churches at Wisley and Pyrford across water meadows and farm land. There are no hills and very few stiles.

Bus: The Green Line bus 715 (Guildford-Kingston-Oxford Circus, half-hourly weekdays and hourly Sundays) stops outside the post office in Ripley village. Cross the road from the post office if coming from Kingston and turn right down a small road between the Craft Centre and a paper shop, cross Ripley Green diagonally right and join the walk from the car park at the cricket pitch.
Car park: There is a small car park behind the shops in the centre of Ripley village, on the right-hand side if coming from Esher, or, if this is full, you can park on the green facing the cricket pitch.
Refreshments: At Ripley or the Anchor Inn about halfway round the walk.

Ripley was once a coaching village and there are still many inns and half-timbered houses dating from Tudor and Elizabethan times. The broad main street has greatly benefited from the opening of the bypass and there are still some signs that it was a gathering point for the London cyclists. The village green has been the scene of cricket matches since the eighteenth century.

From the car park take the wide track across the green with the cricket pitch on the right. You will soon see a large house, Dunsborough Park, on the left, the gardens of which are sometimes open to the public. At the end of some farm cottages, where the track ahead is marked 'Strictly private', bear left on a path which soon crosses the Ockham Mill stream and then at a house go slightly left between holly bushes and over a footbridge and continue to the lock and weir. You may be lucky enough to see herons on this stretch of water meadow.

Cross over the weir and turn right past the lock cottage. Do not go over the small footbridge but continue along the towpath, which lies between the Wey Navigation canal and river Wey for a short distance. The Wey Navigation canal was planned three hundred years ago by Sir Richard Weston of Sutton Place and

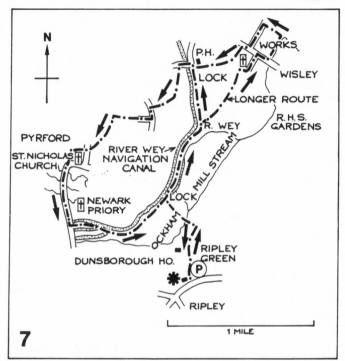

runs between Weybridge and Guildford. The original bridges and locks were built from the ruins of Oatlands Palace in Weybridge.

After about half a mile you reach a footbridge over the canal. If you wish to shorten the walk by 1½ miles continue along the towpath here for another half a mile past many attractively decorated barges and houseboats until the lock and the Anchor public house are reached. Continue from the paragraph marked (A).

For the longer walk climb the stile on the right just past the footbridge and cross the field diagonally right. If the path is indistinct aim for a gatepost in the far hedge, keeping left of two trees in the centre of the field. After passing through the gateposts turn left up the side of the field. You can see the tower of Wisley church in the distance. Keep to the edge of the field on the track and at the top turn right to a gate by a concrete structure. Go up this muddy farm lane for about a quarter of a mile and when the track bends to the left towards the farm keep on past a wooden garage out to a minor road. Turn right to the bridge over the river Wey. Wisley village, which lies beyond the bridge, has been continuously inhabited since prehistoric times. Various excavations at the beginning of the twentieth century have uncovered the site of an ancient British village and a much later group of iron age dwellings. In Weybridge Museum a 12 foot (3.7 m) dugout canoe has been reconstructed from the remains of one found embedded in the riverbank near here.

At the bridge turn left along the towpath by the Wey, which has made a large sweep round past the Royal Horticultural Society's gardens at Wisley to reach this point. When the river bends to the right keep on an asphalt path by the wire fence of the sewage works, and at the gate into the works carry on forward by the fence. This path leads out to the road, where you bear right and almost immediately left through an iron gate to the beautiful little church. The church, dating from the twelfth century, has many interesting features and a board, showing the list of incumbents, indicates that the Black Prince was patron of the living in the fourteenth century.

Pass the church on the left and bear left round the end to a small copse and over a stile. Cross the farmyard to another stile. The line of the path is diagonally left across the field to a wooden bridge but if the field is wet follow the track round the edge of the field. Go over the planked bridge and continue up another field, keeping the hedge on the right. There are fine views of the Surrey hills here. Pass through an iron gate and cross the field diagonally right to the Anchor public house, emerging on to the towpath by the lock.

(A) The two walks continue together from here. At the Anchor turn left across the bridge, passing a notice about the footpath being moved 200 yards, continue along the road to the public footpath sign on the left and take the track across a well kept field of various vegetables. Turn right on a track towards a small greenhouse, emerging on to a road. Turn left and after a short distance turn right down Elveden Close. At the end of this road take a footpath over a stile to the right of a house. This path is rather overgrown in the summer but fortunately is quite short. There is a rather unusual farm notice at the end of the path.

Turn left at the end of the footpath and continue on the track between fields, which soon crosses a muddy farmyard and emerges on to a road. Turn left up to St Nicholas's church, Pyrford, which is set on a low knoll overlooking the ruins of Newark Priory. The church is Norman, complete and virtually unspoilt, with a Tudor porch. The interior has a marvellous timbered roof, the pews are fifteenth-century and the pulpit Jacobean. Opposite the nave is a wall painting dating from 1140. Go through the churchyard with the church on the left, down the gravel path and out on to the road once more. After about a quarter of a mile, passing the ruins of Newark Priory, founded in the middle of the twelfth century, on the left, walk to the traffic lights and turn left down the towpath. The watermill that used to be here was burned to the ground in 1966. The site of a prehistoric village of about 1500 BC was discovered near Pyrford Lock in 1926.

Cross the canal at the lock and continue along the towpath, the haunt of many fishermen. On reaching the lock and weir again, turn right and retrace the last half mile back to the car park at Ripley or to the buses.

8. Wisley Common and Ockham Common

Distance: 8 or 4 miles.
Grid reference: 068582.
Ordnance Survey maps: 1:50,000 sheet 187; 1:25,000 sheet TQ05.

A walk through the pinewoods of Wisley and Ockham commons, visiting the semaphore tower at Chatley Heath, which was last used to relay messages to the fleet at Portsmouth in 1848. The shorter walk goes on to skirt the large lake of Bolder Mere whilst the longer walk goes across fields and through woods past the villages of Martyrs Green and Ockham before crossing the A3 to Ockham Mill and the river Wey, finally traversing a small section of the Royal Horticultural Gardens at Wisley back to the car park.

Trains: The nearest station is at Effingham Junction, which is about a mile from point A on the longer walk, adding two miles to that walk. Turn left from the station and at the road junction turn right and immediately left. After nearly a mile, turn left at the second bridlepath, just before the hamlet of Mays Green.
Bus: The Green Line buses 710 and 715 (Oxford Circus to Guildford) stop outside the Wisley Gardens turning on the A3. Walk up the road towards Wisley Gardens and at the fork just before the gardens keep right for about 70 yards to a small clearing on the right.
Car park: Take the RHS Wisley Gardens turning off the A3 (if approaching from Esher, continue past the turning to the next junction and cross under the bypass to return to Wisley Gardens). Shortly after turning down towards Wisley Gardens, take the right-hand fork and after about 70 yards turn off the road into a

small clearing on the right.

Refreshments: On the longer walk, there are the Black Swan public house at Martyrs Green and the village Post Office and Stores at Ockham.

The walk starts by taking the main track marked by a single post at the rear of the clearing, just left of centre. Continue down this track, crossing a small stream, until you come to a large junction of paths. Take the second wide track on the left and after about 200 yards bear off to the right on the sandy path. In another 50 yards, turn left between silver birches and cross a stream almost immediately. Continue on this track for about half a mile soon with fields on the right. Wisley Common was once mined for iron and is still covered in parallel trenches. Near the main road is a tree-covered barrow at Cock Crow Hill, which was opened in the early twentieth century and showed signs of a cremation thousands of years old.

On reaching a house on a corner where the path forks, turn right and at the end of the garden turn right again with a field on the right past some camping grounds. (The M25 is scheduled to be built at this point and the footpath will be altered slightly to take the path up to the footbridge over the motorway. Do not cross the motorway but follow the new footpath which shortly joins up with the old path.) Continue on this track past a house on the right and a pond on the left. Just before the main road, go past the turning on the left to the car park and take the next track leading to a new footbridge over the A3. Continue forward to pass some wooden bars on the left and immediately cross over a track, shortly to reach a clearing. Carry on in the same direction and, when a wide track soon runs parallel on the left, take a short path through the trees to join it and turn right towards a very large clearing with heather in the centre, bounded by posts.

With the clearing on the right, continue forward past seats until you come to a wide sandy track about halfway round (opposite a path across the centre). Turn left up this wide track and when the track bends to the left continue forward on a smaller switchback path until you reach the top of Telegraph Hill and the Chatley Heath semaphore tower. In the early nineteenth century the Admiralty used a line of thirteen similar hilltop semaphore stations to send messages to Portsmouth, a distance of 68 miles. There was a large post on the top with jointed arms used to send the messages.

Continue past the tower and take the path straight ahead to some wooden posts. Turn left and after about 50 yards turn right on a small track. Take the first turning on the right. There are several fine redwood trees here, one being in the middle of the path. At a bridlepath sign to Hatchford the walks divide.

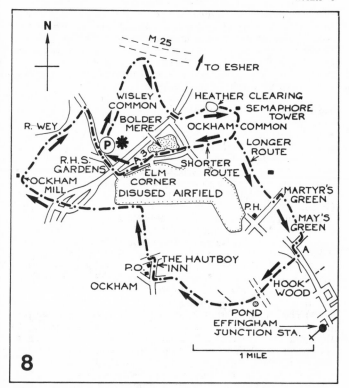

8

For the shorter walk (4 miles)

At the signpost continue forward to a T junction by a single Scots pine, and turn left, soon coming to a large junction of paths. Keep straight on along a wide track and at the next clearing, with a seat and litter basket, continue forward on a small path. At a large pine with three branches curving out from a single trunk turn right and at a T junction turn left. On reaching a car park on the right, go over a wooden planked bridge and turn left through the car park. Cross the road to a path by a post and continue forward to skirt the beautiful lake of Bolder Mere on the right. Cross an extended plank bridge and keep in the same forward direction across all tracks, through the trees to join a rutted lane. Turn right and after some way the lane joins a metalled road. There is a wooden gable of a cottage, festooned with heads of wild animals, a short distance up the road to the left, at the edge of the hamlet of Elm Corner. However, continue forward on the road, eventually passing the disused Wisley Aerodrome, used for experimental flights during the Second World War, but now the large hangars and other buildings have been dismantled. At the entrance to the aerodrome, turn right to the A3. Cross to the Wisley Gardens turning opposite and the bus stop, or on to where the car is parked.

For the longer walk (8 miles)

At the bridlepath sign to Hatchford, turn left and then right at the next fork, coming out on to a lane with some cottages and a farm on the right. Turn left down the lane for about a quarter of a mile, passing Hatchford School on the left. When the lane gives way to a small road, turn left past Flower Cottage. (The Black Swan public house is a short way down the road to the right.) After passing Flower Cottage in the small village of Martyrs Green, cross the road and mount some steps to reach an enclosed path through a kissing gate which leads to a cat hotel on the left. Continue forward on a gravelly drive with fine views ahead and to the left. When the drive swings to the left, keep forward across a field to a public footpath sign and follow a rather brambly path with a fence on the right. Soon cross a small field out on to a road over a two-barred fence. This is the hamlet of Mays Green. Turn right and at the main road turn left. After about 200 yards cross the road to a bridleway on the right.

(A) Those coming from the station join the walk here. Keep to the main bridleway, soon crossing a brick bridge and bearing to the right. This path crosses a grassy ride and eventually emerges at the corner of a field. Continue forward with a ditch on the right and on reaching a concrete path keep on in the same direction past some cottages on the right to a public footpath sign by a gate. Go past a small pond on the left and through a five-barred gate. Take the middle path opposite, marked 'PF no horses'. Continue on this path for several hundred yards until you come to a small but definite pathlet, immediately before a clump of rhododendrons on the left. Carry on along this rather overgrown path and after a while a field borders on the left. The path wanders about to some extent at this point, but keeping the field a few yards to the left you enter a copse and in a short time reach the edge of a large field.

Turn right along the top of the field to a dividing ditch between two fields. Turn left and walk down the field with the ditch on the right to an opening in the field boundary. Continue on down the next field with a hedge on the left. Turn right along the bottom of the field and out through an opening at the corner on to a cart track. After passing some new houses on the right, go out on to a lane and past some delightful old cottages to reach a road, with

Ockham post office on the corner opposite. Ices and sweets are sold here.

Turn right along the road to the Hautboy inn on the corner. Turn left past the inn and after a few yards cross the road to the footpath opposite. Go past the farm and up the track, eventually reaching a field. Make for the stile ahead and cross the gully to climb up the bank to a gate and stile leading into a field. Go straight across the field, making for a concrete stile, which is just over the skyline. Turn left immediately over another stile to take the path enclosed by wire fences which borders the old disused Wisley Aerodrome. (If this path is very overgrown, keep along the top of the field with the wire fence on the right.) At the end of this enclosed path negotiate some rather slippery steps down into a sunken way. Turn right, and, just before the top of a rise, turn left over a two-barred fence. Cross the field to a stile and, keeping a wire fence on the left, continue along the edge of the fields until the bypass comes into view. After passing a derelict cowshed on the left, go over a stile and continue forward to the slip road to the bypass. Turn left and cross the road. Go under the bypass via the footpath. Turn right and cross the road to the small road called Mill Lane.

Just before Ockham Mill at the end of the lane, turn right by a footpath sign and continue past some bungalows and on across the large field with first a fence on the left. Cross a stile in the hedge and over another field to a stile leading to a path which first skirts Wisley Gardens and then goes through a lovely corner of the gardens with some fine specimen trees and the river Wey on the left. The Royal Horticultural Gardens at Wisley were established in 1904 and the grounds cover some 200 acres (81 ha) of land. At the end of the path, cross the stile and a service road and turn right down the minor road back to the car park on the left and out to the main road for the bus. For the station turn into the clearing just before the fork to the gardens and continue from the first paragraph.

9. Holmbury St Mary, Ewhurst and Peaslake

Distance: 7½ miles.
Grid reference: 104451.
Ordnance Survey maps: 1:50,000 sheet 187; 1:25,000 sheets TQ14 and TQ04.

This walk has fine viewpoints from Holmbury and Pitch Hills and the picturesque villages of Ewhurst and Peaslake are visited.

Some of the footpaths and bridleways are likely to be muddy in wet weather.

Bus: The Alder Valley 273 (Guildford via Cranleigh to Ewhurst) stops by the village green in Ewhurst. Start the walk from the paragraph marked (*). The Rambler Bus Service 417 (only on Sundays and public holidays from April to October) travels from Dorking, Leith Hill, Ewhurst, Peaslake, Gomshall, Holmbury St Mary, Wotton and Westcott back to Dorking and can be picked up anywhere en route at a set fare for the day.
Car: There is space for about a dozen or more cars outside the youth hostel at Holmbury St Mary. Turn off the A25 on to the B2126 and just before the village of Holmbury St Mary take a small turning on the right signposted Radnor Lane and Wood-house Lane (also marked with a small YHA sign). Keep on this narrow lane until it peters out at Hurtwood Common.
Refreshments: Inns and general shops at Ewhurst and Peaslake.

Just beyond the car park outside Holmbury St Mary youth hostel, take the path to the right of the larger of the two notices saying 'Hurtwood Control'. On reaching a wide sandy track turn left, and soon cross a wide track. After about a quarter of a mile, after passing a small crossing track and a turning left, branch off left on a wide grassy path. Go over two crossing tracks and at a fork bear left on a sandy track through a wood. Keep ahead when a track comes in from the right. This path leads out to Holmbury Hill with its memorial stone seat and magnificent panorama across to the South Downs. Holmbury Hill is the site of a large iron age fortress and the two ditches, which once had a stockade between them, can still be seen surrounding all but the steep south-facing slope.

With your back to the memorial seat, walk south to take a narrow, very steep path to the right of a wooden post. This path will probably be slippery after rain but easier alternatives can be found on the right-hand side of the path. At the end of the slope, one emerges at a road with a cottage on the right. Turn right past this delightful cottage and its neighbours and at the end of a brick wall on the left cross the road and take a small path between hedges on the right-hand edge of a grassy area. This enclosed path leads down to some wooden steps out to a road, where you turn left and then immediately right on a track. Just past the house, by the pond, branch off to the left along a muddy track. At a games court on the right, go over a stile on the left to enter a field. Cross this field to a gate at the bottom and cross the next field at right angles to a stile just to one side of a tree with farm buildings behind it. Cross this next stile and continue in single file (if crops are growing) slightly left to yet another stile. Go across the fourth

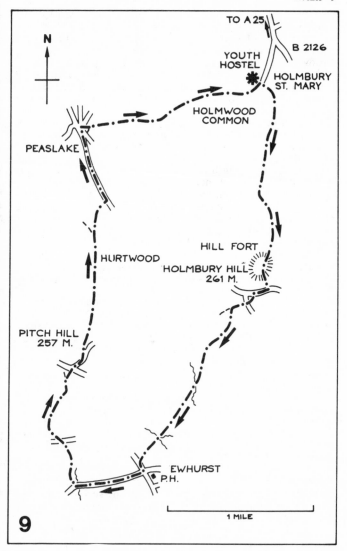

N

TO A 25

B 2126

YOUTH
HOSTEL

HOLMBURY
ST. MARY

HOLMWOOD
COMMON

PEASLAKE

HILL FORT

HOLMBURY HILL
261 M.

HURTWOOD

PITCH HILL
257 M.

EWHURST
P.H.

1 MILE

9

33

field to a stile and over a planked bridge and continue forward again with trees and a ditch on the left. Enter a copse over a stile and soon cross a farm track. Continue forward with a field on the right. Follow the yellow waymarks over the stile and go along beside a field with iron railings on the right. At the end of the field go over another stile and follow the path through the wood. At the road turn left to the beautiful village green at Ewhurst, with an inn, the Boar's Head, on the left. The old but much restored church at Ewhurst is a short way down the road from the green.

(*)From the inn, cross the village green and go down a small road by the side of the garage. Ignore a turning off on the left, and after about half a mile, just after crossing a stream, turn right on a footpath over a stile. Shortly, on the right, there is a large patch of foxgloves which is a marvellous show of colour in June and July. At the end of the field, follow the path round through the swing gate and continue on the rather overgrown path. Go over the stile by the gate, turn left down the road, and turn right at the first turning. When the metalled track sweeps round to enter a private forecourt, go ahead on the bridleway through the trees. After a house on the right, turn sharply right through white metal posts to reach the road. Cross to the road opposite and go up this road past some houses on the right.

At a fork, take the left-hand, unmade-up track going uphill. Follow this track for about three quarters of a mile, soon coming to the ridge of Pitch Hill, where there are marvellous views on either side since the trees have been cut down. When the broad sandy track bears off to the left, turn right towards a gate leading into a wood. Do not enter the wood, but turn left to follow the path downhill with the wood and fence on the right. This path leads out to a grassy verge by a house on the right. Follow the stony path out to the road and turn left for about half a mile to the village of Peaslake.

Just before the cross in Peaslake village, turn right for a few yards up the road and then turn left by a garage to a house, up a steep path. At the top, on reaching wooded common land, continue forward downhill. Cross over a track and go under a bar, or over a very low stile, and after some way, on coming to a fork, take the left-hand branch. Cross a stile and keep ahead over three crossing tracks. Continue forward when a path comes in on the left. Keep on the main sunken path and, after going down into a clearing, still keep on the main path going slightly uphill. Go over a crossing track and maintain the same direction back to the car park by Holmbury St Mary youth hostel.

10. Great Bookham Common and Effingham Common

Distance: 7½ or 4 miles.
Grid reference: 130557.
Ordnance Survey maps: 1:50,000 sheet 187; 1:25,000 sheets TQ15 and TQ05.

A walk over Great and Little Bookham commons, which comprise over 400 acres (162 ha) of oak and holly owned by the National Trust. The walk continues through woods and fields and there are plenty of blackberries to be picked in season along the hedgerows. Some of the stiles may be in a dilapidated condition and the bridlepaths on the commons will be muddy after rain.

Trains: From Bookham station turn left towards the sharp bend in the road. The walk starts from the car park at Commonside on the left.
Bus: The bus stops outside Bookham station.
Car park: Turn off the A246 towards Great Bookham and continue on to the station. The car park is at Commonside, which is on a sharp bend just before the station.
Refreshments: In Great Bookham.

From the car park walk up towards the railway line and by the bridge fork right along a metalled track. When this track ends by some houses on the right, continue ahead a short way and at a junction of paths by a bungalow turn sharply left on a grassy path for a few yards, cross over a path and continue forward on a bridleway. Keep on this path for about half a mile, passing several ponds on the left. At a large clearing by a house, continue forward past the house and turn left down a track marked with blue posts. At the next junction of paths continue on a grassy track to the left. Carry on past the white house on the left and, after crossing the river Mole, which is only a small stream here, ignore the immediate turning on the right to a house and take the next turning on the right up a grassy track a short way to a stile leading into a large field. The walks divide at this point.

For the longer walk (7½ miles)

Cross the large field past two trees in the centre and make for a double stile in the hedge, just to the right of the two trees. The line of the path is now across the middle of the next field to a stile opposite, but if the field is cultivated turn left down the side of the field and skirt the edge of the field to the stile, which was in a very poor condition when we did the walk. On the other side of this stile turn right and follow the hedge bounding the field towards a railway arch in the distance.

Go through the arch and follow the drive past the farm down to the road. Cross this to the footpath sign opposite. The path through the wood is rather overgrown. After some way, bear right at a U-shaped junction and in about 200 yards, just before a pond, take a small pathlet on the right. Fallen trees are rather hazardous here but the path soon reaches a stile. Continue forward with a hedge on the right to a sandy track which leads to a large gate. There is a stile in the hedge to the right of the gate out on to the road. Turn left for about 200 yards and take the path on the right by the sign 'Barnsthorns'. Bear right at the bend by a public footpath notice and bear left immediately. Cross the footbridge and go over a stile into a field. Continue round the edge of the field with lots of bramble bushes on the right. At the entrance to the next field, continue on a path across the corner of the field. At the next hedge turn right on to a path between hedges. Keep on this path, with fine views to the left, and eventually cross a track leading to a large modern house on the right. Continue on this enclosed path for some way. Bear left when a footpath comes in on the right. Take the first left turn into the rhododendron and pine woods called the Blue Ride.

Follow this path through the woods for some distance and at a crossing path keep on in the direction shown by the public footpath signs. At the bottom of the slope turn left and keep to the path with a field on the right. This path leads out to a road known as The Drift. Turn left and follow the road past the Drift golf course and clubhouse out to Forest Road. Turn right over the railway bridge and then sharp left down Forest Lane, with bungalows on the right. Bear left at a small grassy island in the road. Just before Effingham Common turn right at a public footpath sign through the trees. When the path becomes rather overgrown, bear left on a path out on to the common. Turn right and follow the path with the wood on the right. At the top of the wood, with the road ahead, turn right, still with the wood on the right. At the end of a cultivated field turn left on a small path with a ditch on the left, towards a belt of trees ahead. Continue on this path round the cricket pitch on to a stony track. Turn left down to the road. Turn right for a short distance to turn left down Lower Farm Road.

For the shorter walk (4 miles)

From the stile go towards two trees standing alone in the centre of the field. At the trees turn left towards a stile in the hedge. Cross over the stile and turn right down the path. After a National Trust sign, take the first turning on the left through some woods. Cross over a stream and go over the stile into a field.

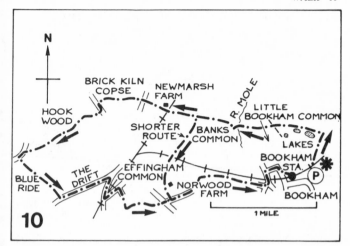

Keep straight ahead parallel to a small stream running through the field and cross the railway line by the stiles. Continue forward to the end of the next field with a wood ahead, cross a stile and go along the small path with the fine garden of Norwood Farm on the left. This red brick house is thought to have been built six hundred years ago by a Bishop of Winchester as the residence of a bailiff. Cross another stile out on to a small lane, turn left, passing the tithe barn of 103 feet (31 m), and follow the lane to a small common just before the road. Turn left along the edge of the common to join the longer walk at Lower Farm Road.

The two walks continue together as follows. Go down this attractive residential road and at the end climb over the iron ladder into a large field with horses and some large lakes to the far right. Turn left towards the wire fence and at the fence turn right, keeping the fence on the left. Cross the stile at the lower end of the field and continue in the same direction with the fence now on the right. Cross another stile (the fence is on the left again) and continue to the end of the field. Climb over the large concrete stile and turn immediately left to make for a small path between the railway line and the farm. This enclosed path leads out to a small road. Turn left and cross the railway bridge and follow the road to a large hotel on the corner. Turn right past the hotel and at a sharp bend in the road to the right take the grassy path leading across the common straight ahead. When Bookham station soon appears ahead, go along the path leading towards the station and cross the footbridge into the station yard and out to the road for the bus stop. Turn left for the car park.

37

11. Oxshott, Fairmile Common and Claygate

Distance: 8 or 5 miles.
Grid reference: 142611.
Ordnance Survey maps: 1:50,000 sheet 187; 1:25,000 sheet TQ06/16.

This walk crosses some very beautiful commons in the Esher and Claygate area and the full walk briefly passes the edge of Chessington Zoo with a glimpse of some of the animals there. Some of the paths in the woods will be muddy after rain but the walk is suitable for all seasons and is especially lovely in frosty weather.

Trains: Oxshott station. Walk up towards the Esher-Leatherhead road from the station and go through a gap in the metal fence on the left to the car park, where the walk begins.
Bus: The Mole Valley Leatherhead to Esher bus stops just outside the road leading to Oxshott station. The walk starts from the car park just inside the common.
Car park: The car park is on the right of the Esher-Oxshott-Leatherhead road, coming from Esher, just before the sign to Oxshott station and the railway bridge.
Refreshments: There is a cafe by the railway line on Oxshott Heath or the Winning Horse at Claygate is passed on the full walk.

The walk starts from the car park on Oxshott Common, which is just before the little road leading to Oxshott station. By a white single-bar gate stopping cars from parking on the common, turn right on the main path leading up the hill. At the top of the slope turn left towards the war memorial and continue along the escarpment, which is provided with seats to admire the fine views across to Fetcham. Descend the steps at the end of the escarpment and turn right at the crossing track. Continue forward across another track until some houses are reached. Go straight ahead through some concrete posts and iron bars to a passage between the houses to the left of another passage, crossing the road after a few yards to a passage opposite. This leads past Reeds School on the left with its fine buildings and playing fields. When the path ends at the corner of a road, continue ahead past a thatched house on the left. Turn right at the end of the road and after about 50 yards turn right down Sandy Lane. At the end of the houses on the right there is a footpath which closely follows the road. At a bend in the road to the right cross the road to a small

38

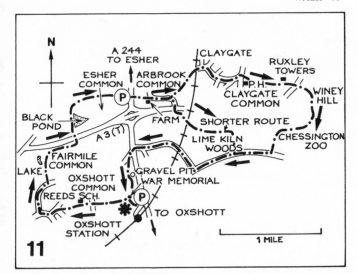

car park at Fairmile Common.

Take the first path on the right through some posts and at a fork keep to the right. On reaching a crossing track, marked 'Horse ride', turn right along it. Cross a small stream in a rhododendron dell and climb the slope the other side. Cross over a path and continue along the top of a mossy slope, which soon passes a beautiful lake in the hollow. Just before reaching the fence to the Esher bypass, turn right and walk along the top of a small bank, which eventually comes out to a bridlepath. Turn left down this and cross the bypass by the footbridge. Turn left and take the first turning on the right through a wooden barrier. After a short while you pass the very lovely Black Pond with its improvised swimming pool and changing rooms in the woods. Go through some wooden bars and on reaching a crossing path turn right and follow the clear track through the trees. Go under some wooden posts and continue forward. At a wide junction of paths, take the second path on the left by a green concrete post. Cross two wide horse rides and just before a wooden barrier near the bypass turn half-left. At a crossing track turn left and continue towards a car park on the right by Copsem Lane, which can be seen in the distance.

Make your way through the car park and cross Copsem Lane to a small path in the wood opposite. Skirt a small pond on the left, turn half-right, and continue in a forward direction for about 100 yards until you reach a horse ride with jumps across it. After some

39

way, just before the bypass, turn left at a crossing track, go over a little bridge and continue down a definite path out on to a small road at a corner by a seat. Continue forward past Arbrook Farm and some cottages on the right until reaching a junction of paths. This is where the walks divide.

For the shorter walk (5 miles)

At the junction of paths take the first turning on the right down a sandy track between fields. Go under the bypass by means of the tunnel and keep to the track for about half a mile. If it is very wet, there is a small path on the left in the woods which follows the track closely. On reaching Lime Kiln Woods on the right, take the first definite path through the woods. This path meanders through the wood and eventually reaches Fairoak Lane. Turn right and after a couple of hundred yards turn right down Stokesheath Road. You now rejoin the longer walk at paragraph A.

For the longer walk (8 miles)

At the junction of paths keep on forward through a wooden barrier. At a fork keep right by fields, soon emerging on a lovely path between fields with open views across to Claygate. This path eventually crosses the railway by a bridge on the outskirts of Claygate. Continue up the small road and turn right along Beaconsfield Road. At the end turn left and after a few yards cross the main road. The Winning Horse is on the right here. Go down the small cul-de-sac by the footpath sign and out past the barrier on to Claygate Common. Turn right immediately at a fork and go straight over three crossing tracks. Just before the open green turn left and then right on to the grass. Cross the common diagonally left to a path by some houses through white posts. Continue past some fields with horses on the right and Ruxley Towers on the left. Ruxley Towers is the headquarters of the National Union of General and Municipal Workers. Cross the bypass by the bridge and continue forward on a bridlepath between hedges. Cross the lane at the end to a gate on to open land known as Winey Hill. Turn right and, keeping the hedge on the right, continue up the hill to a double enclosure by the edge of Chessington Zoo. Go through the enclosure, passing the zoo with its spotted deer enclosure. There are fine views here across to Ruxley Towers and the lake by the side of the bypass, which is comparatively new and does not yet appear on the Ordnance Survey map.

Continue forward to a stile leading into Sixty Acre Wood and almost immediately turn right in the wood. After about 100 yards fork left and cross a ride by a jump. On reaching a T junction, after some way along a somewhat muddy track, turn left and when you reach the road clamber up a steep bank on to the road. Turn right here and walk along the grass verge for about a mile until reaching Stokesheath Road on the right. The two walks now continue together.

(A) Turn right down Stokesheath Road and continue along this undulating road with its beautiful houses and lovely views to the right across to Claygate. When the road finally reaches Warren Lane, turn left for about 100 yards to Sandy Lane on the right with a white coal post on the corner of the road. (The coal post, or iron man, with its City of London arms, is a boundary post or coal tax post whose origins go back to Restoration times. In 1667 tolls had to be paid on coal brought into the city and in 1851 the posts were set up at points 20 miles from the GPO but later they were moved and the tolls were abolished in 1889.) Take the path at the corner of the common leading diagonally away between the two roads. When this path reaches the large sand pit, cross the pit and take the path opposite on the left, past a small pond. There is a maze of paths here but if you continue forward, keeping the road well on the left, you will soon reach the car park on Oxshott Common.

12. Mickleham, Leatherhead and Fetcham Downs

Distance: 8½, 6½ or 5 miles.
Grid reference: 171538.
Ordnance Survey maps: 1:50,000 sheet 187; 1:25,000 sheet TQ15.

This is a lovely walk over Mickleham Downs with various alternatives along the Roman Stane Street or over Leatherhead Downs, finishing by crossing Fetcham Downs and Norbury Park, with fine views across the Mole valley. It is suitable for any time of the year. The M25 is scheduled to cross Stane Street and Green Lane on the longest walk but provision will be made to cross the motorway with very little deviation from the original walk.

Trains: Leatherhead station. This adds about another 1½ miles to any of the walks. From the station go down the approach road and cross the road to a footpath opposite by the Randalls Road sign. Cross a small park with the railway line on the right and, after crossing a road, continue parallel to the railway for about a quarter of a mile. At the main road by the roundabout, cross to the Leisure Centre. Bear left between the tennis courts and the football ground and continue through the recreation ground to the river Mole. Turn right and walk along the towpath out through a gate on to a track. Turn right to join the other walks at (*).

Buses: The Green Line bus 714 stops on the A24 just before the turning off to Mickleham.

Car park: The car park is on the right of the A24 (Leatherhead-Dorking road) coming from Leatherhead. There is a break in the barrier of the dual carriageway immediately opposite the turning signposted to Mickleham on the left, and the car park is visible a few yards to the right. From the car park turn left and walk about 100 yards to cross the A24 to a bus stop and telephone kiosk near the sign pointing up the hill to the King William IV public house.

Refreshments: At the King William IV public house (at opening times) and in Leatherhead (on the longest walk).

Walk up the small road by the side of the bus stop, ignoring a right fork almost immediately. Take the footpath up beside the King William IV pub and when this path emerges on to a crossing track by a broken wall, the walks divide. The shorter walk follows very pleasant roads with beautiful houses and the longer walks go over Leatherhead Downs and along Stane Street.

For the shortest walk (5 miles)

Turn left by the broken wall to an iron gate and continue across the junction and on to a fork, where you bear left. Continue on through a white gate and take the next turning on the right up the hill. Turn right up Crabtree Drive by an inset postbox in the wall and eventually emerge on the A246. Cross the road slightly left to a path opposite with posts and follow the attractive lane for about half a mile. Cross the main road and turn right for a short distance. Turn left down Thorncroft Drive and over the river Mole. (For the station turn right down the towpath and retrace your steps to the station.) Continue the walk at the paragraph headed 'All the walks continue here'.

For the longer walks (8½ and 6½ miles)

Cross the track to the small path opposite and climb this attractive sloping path through the trees to a crossing path by some fallen trunks. Turn left and after some way turn right at a T junction, pass by a ruined cottage and go over a stile. This beautiful path leads past Cherkley Court in the valley where there are some of the finest yews in Surrey, one over 20 feet (6.1 m) in girth. At the next stile turn left at a crossing path and keep left when a track comes in on the right. On reaching a wide crossing track, turn left on to Stane Street, which was originally built by the Romans and ran from London to Chichester. Continue on this ancient track until you reach a cross track with a cattle trough in the field on the left. The longer walks divide here.

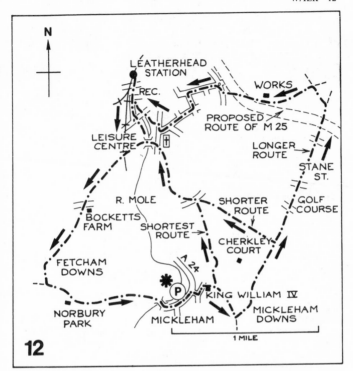

For the longer walk (6½ miles)

Turn left at the cattle trough past a cottage and over a metalled track. Continue on this path, eventually coming to the A246 by the side of a fine house with an indoor swimming pool. Cross the road to a path between posts slightly left and follow the lane for about half a mile. Cross the main road and turn right for a short distance. Turn left down Thorncroft Drive and over the river Mole. (For the station turn right down the towpath and retrace your steps to the station.)

For the longest walk (8½ miles)

Continue along Stane Street at the cattle trough and follow the Street for about another two miles, crossing first the main road with Tyrell's Wood golf course on the right and then over two further roads. (The M25 is due to cross Stane Street a short distance from the second road, but provision will be made for

43

access across the motorway.) Continue along Stane Street until reaching a staggered cross track by fields, then turn left. Ignore a small path on the left and at a wide junction of tracks turn left down a magnificent beech avenue for about half a mile. After passing the extensive Goblin works on the right, turn left and then right on to a path running through a copse. After briefly joining the road at a corner, turn down the wide path known as Green Lane, through the white posts. (Green Lane will cross the M25 just before the junction with the A24 by the Patrol Service Centre; access will be by bridge or tunnel.) On reaching the main road, turn right to the roundabout. Cross by the roundabout to take the road leading down towards Leatherhead town centre. Take the second turning on the left, Fortyfoot Road, and then turn right down Poplar Road. This eventually leads past Leatherhead church on the left, with its five-hundred-year-old church tower, out to the main road. (For the station, turn right and then left down a path just before the Mansion Adult Education College. At the river turn right and follow the path under the bridge, eventually coming out at a road. Turn right by the railway line back to the station.)

Turn left and after a few hundred yards cross the road to Thorncroft Drive on the right. Cross the river Mole.

All the walks continue here

(*)Continue past several industrial firms and the Leatherhead Leisure Centre. Go over a railway bridge and follow the unmade-up track round the edge of a field, over a stile and up the side of another field. Turn left down the other side of the field between hedges and finally out at the bypass. Cross the road to the drive opposite leading to Bocketts Farm, and take the second turning on the right as the drive swings left down to the farm. This path skirts a field and after about half a mile bears round past a barn out to a junction of tracks. Take the small centre track going uphill between bushes with a fine beech tree on the right. At the next crossing track turn left, cross the main track at the bottom of the slope and continue forward uphill past centuries-old beeches and yews. Look out for large London snails, which are the descendants of those brought over by the Romans.

Continue in a forward direction, ignoring all paths to left and right, eventually coming out on to a stony track. Bear left and, on reaching woodcutters' sheds on the right, fork left. At a small lane continue forward on the metalled drive, soon passing Norbury Park House on the right. This house dates from the eighteenth century and is famous for its 'painted room' with walls and ceiling painted with landscapes which blend with the views from the windows. The house now belongs to Surrey County Council.

At a yellow waymarked log, where the fencing by the side of the track bends to the right, turn right down a small path, crossing a metalled track and continuing on, coming out on to a steep grassy slope covered with violets and cowslips in spring and with fine views across to Mickleham Downs, with Leatherhead to the far left and Box Hill to the right. The Mole at Mickleham in dry summers is sometimes an empty river bed, although a mile away at Burford Bridge it is flowing. The reason is that the waters disappear into the chalk and flow along in subterranean clefts, appearing normally again at Leatherhead.

At the bottom of the slope, keep right of the drive on a pathlet in the grass verge which continues down between posts, and where the track bends left for Mickleham Priory continue straight ahead on the path with a fence on the left and the river Mole on the right, to the bridge and the main road.

Turn left for the car park and bus stop. Those starting from Leatherhead station should walk along the A24 for about 100 yards and then cross the road to a bus stop and telephone kiosk by a small road. Continue from the first paragraph.

13. Mickleham Downs, White Hill and Box Hill

Distance: 7½, 4½ or 3 miles.
Grid reference: 171538.
Ordnance Survey maps: 1:50,000 sheet 187; 1:25,000 sheet TQ15.

This is a beautiful walk over Mickleham Downs, along the stretch of grassland known as White Hill, and the longest walk then proceeds to Box Hill with its magnificent views across the Weald to the distant South Downs. This is a hilly walk with at least four ascents (and descents) on the complete walk, two of them being quite steep. The chalky slopes can be rather slippery after rain but this is a walk for any season although the flaming colours of the foliage on the downs in autumn are particularly striking.

Trains: The nearest station is at Box Hill, which is about 1½ miles from the car park on the A24, or the walk could be joined at the Fort tea rooms on the top of Box Hill (this adds about 2 miles to the longest walk). From the station go down the approach road to the A24. Cross by the subway and turn left to the Burford Bridge Hotel. Climb the steep side of Box Hill and at the top turn right on to a chalky track keeping the escarpment on the right. After passing Labelliere's tomb, turn left away from the edge at a fork, and go through some posts to the cafe. Join the walk at paragraph A.

Buses: The Green Line bus 714 stops on the A24 just before the turning off to Mickleham.

Car park: The car park is on the right of the A24 (Leatherhead-Dorking road) coming from Leatherhead. There is a break in the barrier of the dual carriageway immediately opposite the turning signposted to Mickleham on the left, and the car park is visible a few yards to the right. From the car park turn left and after about 100 yards cross the A24 to a bus stop and telephone kiosk near the sign pointing up the hill to the King William IV public house.

Refreshments: At the King William IV public house (at opening times) and on the top of Box Hill when the Fort tea rooms are open (on the longest walk).

Go up the small road by the side of the bus stop and ignore a right fork almost immediately. Take the footpath up the side of the King William IV pub, crossing a track to a small path opposite. This path wends its way up through ancient yews and beeches and when a track comes in on the left bear right just after some large fallen trees. After some way, as you leave the wood at the top, ignore a small path on the right and at the fork take the left, narrower path, crossing over a small track shortly afterwards. There is a wire fence on one's left and fine views across to Cherkley Court and Leatherhead. At a T junction turn left downhill.

After some way, shortly after passing a concrete shed in a hollow on the left, turn right on a rising path, which soon merges with a broad track. On reaching a more open space, turn left and this leads to the wide grassy downland known as White Hill. Turn left to the end of the ride and go past a National Trust signpost, almost immediately branching off to the right just before a nature reserve sign. Keep ahead when the path divides to the right. This beautiful woodland path soon steepens downhill and the last slopes can be slippery after rain. It emerges at a small road by the side of a car park with a cottage opposite.

For the shortest walk (3 miles)

Turn right through the car park and continue on a path with a field on the left. At a junction of paths take the middle one ahead up the steep slope. This most attractive path, after the initial steepness, winds gently above the road amid beautiful yews and beeches for some way and eventually reaches the seat (*) where you turn right and join the other walks.

For the longer walks, cross the road to the bridleway by the side of the cottage and continue up this path with fields on either side.

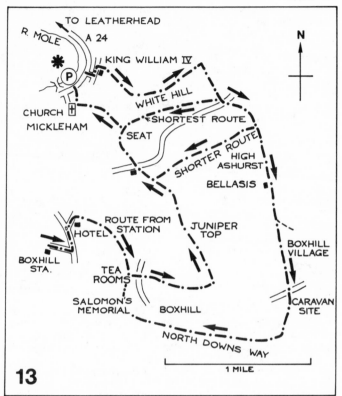

13

At the end of an old flint wall on the right, the longer walks divide.

For the longer walk (4½ miles)

Turn right at the end of the flint wall through a gate on to a metalled road inside the wall. After about half a mile, when this road bends sharply to the right and a track leads off to the left to a gate marked 'Private woodlands', continue forward up a steep slope with some rough steps (hidden by leaves in the autumn) to a stile. This path leads between fences over a barrier to a large field occupied by sheep in the summer. Keeping the fence on one's right proceed in the same direction across the field and cross two stiles bridging a farm track and keep on the path, soon crossing another stile into a wood. At a T junction turn right and keep on

47

the main footpath when a small path joins it. On emerging on to wide open grassland, turn right down to the road with a cottage entrance on the left.

For the longest walk (7½ miles)

At the end of the flint wall, turn left along the metalled road. In the winter there are fine views to the left across to Headley Heath. After passing the entrance to the Ashurst Youth Camp on the right there is a horse ride on the left which closely follows the road but is not suitable in wet weather. Keep on for about a mile, passing Bellasis on the right with its belfry and beautiful double wooden doors. After going between two wooden posts on either side of the road, leave the metalled road at a junction of paths, keeping to the track nearest the woods on the right. The track passes some houses and caravans on the outskirts of Box Hill village and finally comes out on a road with the 'Roof of the World' caravan site across the road on the left. Cross the road to the footpath opposite and follow the path past a riding school on the right until it joins the North Downs Way, denoted by the acorn sign. The disused Brockham Quarries can be seen on the left. Follow the acorn signs down some nine staggered steps across the path and then turn sharply to the right up some steps and a steep slope with a hand rail, still following the North Downs Way. On reaching a track at a horseshoe bend, take the right-hand path leading uphill. At a gate turn left down some steps and follow the acorn signs and white marks on the trees, eventually coming out on the fine escarpment of Box Hill. Walk along the open downland, keeping the road on your right, until you reach the pulpit on Box Hill built in memory of Leopold Salomons of Norbury Park, who gave Box Hill to the nation in 1914. The famous view here over the Weald to Chanctonbury Ring and the South Downs is unforgettable.

(A) The Fort tea rooms are a little way further on and those coming from Box Hill station join the walk here. From the cafe cross to the car park opposite and continue across the green to another car park by the side of the road. Keeping the road on the right, follow a faint track in the woods and cross a rough drive leading to a house. Turn half-left and continue forward, ignoring a track on the left. At a crossing track turn left and almost at once take the right-hand fork, soon reaching a track by the corner of a caravan park. Turn left and keep left at the next fork. After about 200 yards turn right at a holly clump and on reaching a sloping T junction with a large yew on the right bear left. Ignore a main track on the left. At a crossing path turn left and keep on through a beautiful avenue of trees until you reach a grassy track between silver birches. This leads to the open downland called Juniper Top with fine views across to Mickleham Downs and beyond. Keep ahead on the open slope downhill, eventually entering a wooded area. Go under a wooden bar into Juniper Bottom and emerge at a small road by a cottage.

The longer walks continue together. Cross the road and climb the very steep slope opposite to a fork at the top. Bear to the right on the main path in an uphill direction until you reach a well placed seat with fine views across the valley to Ranmore church.

(*)**The shortest walk** now joins the other walks by turning right at the seat. The longer walks turn left at the seat. At a black iron corner post turn left and after about 25 yards fork left by a yew tree and keep on the main path, which drops down to a wide track (Stane Street). Cross to the 'squeeze' in the wire fence ahead and follow the path downhill. Continue forward through some iron posts enclosing a path on the left. Cross the stile at the end of the path and turn left along a gravelled drive to take the second gate on the right through the churchyard by the beautiful Mickleham church.

Keep on forward on a path between a fence and a hedge crossing a track to a path opposite. Follow this to the main road for the bus stop and car park opposite. For Box Hill station do not cross the main road but continue right to the sign to the King William IV pub at the start of the walk.

14. South Holmwood and Anstiebury Farm

Distance: 7 or 5 miles.
Grid reference: 172451.
Ordnance Survey maps: 1:50,000 sheet 187; 1:25,000 sheet TQ14.

A walk over Holmwood Common to Fourwents Pond and then along fields and woodland paths up to Anstiebury Farm on the Redland Heights, where there are splendid views across Surrey. The longer walk continues along the Heights and then down to cross the main road to Holmwood Common, whilst the shorter walk returns to the car park via South Holmwood.

Trains: From Holmwood station turn left and take the first turning on the left, Moorhurst Lane, to join the walk at (*).
Buses: Buses from Dorking stop near the war memorial in South Holmwood on the A24. Turn up Mill Road to join the walk at the car park.
Car park: On the A24, Dorking to Horsham road, take the turning, Mill Road, on the left from Dorking in South Holmwood

village and park in the small car park almost immediately on the right near the cricket pitch.
Refreshments: Public houses on the A24.

From the car park cross Mill Road to take the path slightly to the right of the public footpath sign, with a ditch running alongside. After about a quarter of a mile, when the hedge and drive of a house appear ahead, turn left on to a smaller path over a plank bridge. Ignoring a left fork immediately, keep forward on the rising path and cross a drive to take a small path to the left of the house ahead. After passing a pond cross over a track and carry on forward a short distance up to a T junction. Turn right along a grassy track, cross a horse ride and immediately turn right down a wide grassy track parallel to the horse ride. Follow this wide track over a planked stream to a horse barrier at the end. Go through a gap in the barrier and turn right downhill to cross a planked stream. Take the path to the left of the telegraph pole and cross a wide track to a small path opposite.

This path soon swings to the left and runs parallel to a small stream. Ignoring a side path to the stream, cross the stream at the next fork and continue forward a few yards to another fork. Take the right-hand path slightly uphill to a small crossing track. Turn left by a holly bush towards the attractive Fourwents Pond, with plenty of seats for picnickers. At the pond turn right through the car park to Mill Road.

Turn right along Mill Road for a short distance and then turn left down a drive marked with a public bridleway sign. At the end of the houses climb over a stile to continue on the path between fields. After crossing a brick bridge over a stream carry on up the slope of the field on a small indistinct grassy path. At the top of the slope bear half-right to a small gate in the line of trees about 75 yards from the railway line. (If the field is planted with crops continue to the stile by the railway line and follow the edge of the field round to the gate.) Go through the gate and at the crossing track turn right. At some cottages bordering a small green, join a made-up lane to the main road ahead.

Cross the dual carriageway to a small road slightly to the left, signposted Beare Green. After a short way turn right down Moorhurst Lane.

(*)After about half a mile, just after a drive down to a house on the left, fork left and continue on this track for another quarter of a mile. Just past a rusty gate lying in the wood and before a stream, turn right on to a small path through a copse carpeted with bluebells in spring, a beautiful sight. At the end of the wood cross a cart track to a stile opposite.

Climb up the side of the field, keeping the hedge on the right, to a stile in the top right-hand corner. Cross the stile and follow

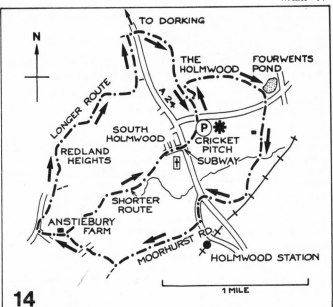

14

the path across the middle of the field to a stile by the edge of a wood. Continue along the path through the beechwood with a wire fence on the right. Where the track bears left carry on ahead up to another stile. Cross the field diagonally right to a stile situated to the right of some farm buildings on the skyline. This is Anstiebury Farm and the walks diverge here.

For the shorter walk (5 miles)

Turn right along the rough farm track with its superb views and by the entrance to a house called Taresmocks cross a stile in the holly hedge. Continue down this path, which eventually comes out on to a small road. Turn left along it to the main road, ignoring a road to the left and passing the church away on the right. Cross under the main road by means of the subway, climb the steps past the war memorial and continue round the cricket pitch to the car park.

For the longer walk (7 miles)

Turn left through the farm and at the minor road turn right to a T junction. Turn right and after a short distance turn right on to a rising path. Continue on this path ignoring side turnings. At a large water tank at a meeting of paths, take the third path from the left, going downhill and bending right almost immediately. At two tracks off to the left take the first one bending round to the left like a horseshoe. Keep on the upper path at a fork. At a large crossing track turn right and enter a wood on a narrow path going downhill. At a small crossing path turn right and after a few yards take the left fork going downhill. Keep going down and when the path bends sharply left take the small path ahead through the wood. This path twists and turns through the wood, eventually coming out by some telegraph poles with fields ahead. Turn left along the line of the poles and on coming to a field keep on the path in the woods which closely follows the edge of the field. On reaching a bridleway follow this down to some cottages, bending round the hedge of a cottage on to a cinder track, which leads down to the main road.

Cross the main road to the bridleway opposite on Holmwood Common. After crossing a planked stream bear right at a T junction and then fork right on to a small path to the right of an oak tree. At a wide crossing track turn right towards the football pitch. At the end of the pitch take the wide grassy path ahead towards a metal barrier. Go under the barrier and turn right after about 200 yards at the first crossing track, leading downhill into a gully. Cross the stream and climb up the other side. This track soon joins the outward path to return to the car park. For the station, turn left on joining the path and continue from the first paragraph of the walk when the hedge and drive of a house appear ahead.

15. Highridge Wood, Brockham and Betchworth

Distance: 7½ miles.
Grid reference: 198470.
Ordnance Survey maps: 1:50,000 sheet 187; 1:25,000 sheets TQ14, TQ24.

A delightful walk through woodland and fields to Brockham, then on to the outskirts of Betchworth, returning via Gadbrook. There are no hills to climb and for the most part it is easy walking country except for some rather dilapidated stiles, but some mud will be encountered in the winter months. Many of the footpaths are across farm land and care should be taken not to damage any of the crops and to keep dogs under control.

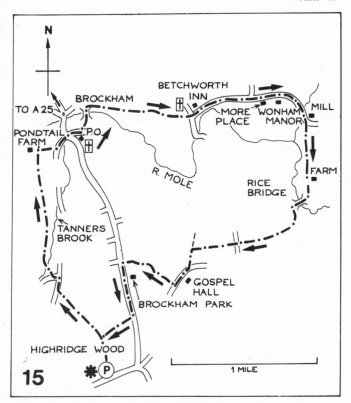

Bus: 439 (Newdigate-Redhill) and 449. No services on Sunday. The nearest bus stop is at the crossroads about 1½ miles south of Brockham. Turn right at the crossroads and after a few hundred yards turn right to the Forestry Commission car park in Highridge Wood.

Car park: In Highridge Wood. Take the road to Brockham from the A25 and at a crossroads 1½ miles south of Brockham turn right. The car park is a few hundred yards down the road on the right.

Refreshments: Inns and shops at Brockham and an inn at Betchworth.

In the Forestry Commission car park in Highridge Wood, take the main track opposite the car park entrance through the dark

53

pinewood. At the end of the wood by some wooden posts cross the clearing to a wide track opposite. Continue ahead on this track and after a while cross a stile on to a smaller grassy path. Ignoring a small path off to the right, take the second grassy path right and on entering the trees keep ahead on a narrow path by a ditch. At a crossing track by a bridleway post, turn left and shortly enter a field through an old wooden gate. Keep forward along the right-hand edge of the field by the hedge and go through a gate on to a rough track leading past a house by a lane. Turn right, and then left down a small road past a farm. At a corner of the lane, shortly before a cottage on the right, turn right through a gate on a rough track across a field. Cross Tanners Brook and bear off diagonally right to a gate and stile in the corner of the field. Now keep ahead along the edge of various fields, crossing over some stiles and other barriers, until you come to a farm track by a farm. Turn right towards Brockham and at the road turn left, shortly crossing a bridge, into Brockham village, with its beautiful green and picturesque cottages and inns. This is one of the most photographed village cricket greens in England and W. G. Grace is said to have played there. On Guy Fawkes night a huge bonfire and fireworks display are held on the green.

Cross the road to a small road opposite, past the Royal Oak and Duke's Head public houses, and shortly take the public bridleway ahead to the left of a drive to a house. Cross the river Mole and keep to the right along the lane. At a fork by a hedge, keep right past some back gardens at first, with the river below on the right. At the end of a field cross to a footpath ahead and at some farm buildings keep ahead past a notice saying 'Beware of the bull'. This path leads past Betchworth church and through an arch to a lane.

Cross to the road opposite with the Dolphin inn on the corner. Follow this road for about a mile, passing More Place, a restored fifteenth-century house with a stone chimneystack at the north end, and soon glimpsing Wonham Manor with its battlements. At Wonham Mill on the left, turn right over a very narrow foot-bridge over the Mole. Follow the path through the woods, cross a stile and keep along a wire fence bordering the river. Here the first of at least four pillboxes can be seen on the left. Turn left along the riverside and follow the path up between telegraph posts. Cross a stile and continue along the path on the left-hand side of the field, past a further pillbox, and skirt a farm garden. Cross a cattle grid to a wooden five-barred gate ahead with bars on both sides. Turn right along the sunken path, which leads to the river once more by the fourth pillbox.

Cross the river by the concrete bridge and take the footpath slightly uphill ahead. Climb the two-barred barrier into a large field and keep to the right-hand edge of the field. At the top of the field turn left and continue along to a footpath sign in the far corner by a wood. Follow the sign left to an iron gate and track into a wood. At the far end of the wood keep along the right-hand side of a field to a stile in the corner out on to a small road. Cross slightly left to a footpath sign opposite and continue across the middle of this large field. At a cart track halfway across the field, the path should, strictly speaking, continue in the same direction but, if the land is planted with crops and there is no visible path, one should turn right here down to a small wood and then left along the bottom of the field. On reaching a track turn left up towards a house on the far edge of the field. At the house continue on a track leading to a road with a chapel opposite. Turn right and in a short distance turn right again at a public footpath sign. At a cottage ahead take a small footpath on the left past a garage, cross a stile and keep along the right-hand hedgerow to a rather hidden stile in the corner of the field. Cross this stile and immediately cross another to take an enclosed path on the left to a further stile. Continue ahead along the left-hand edge of a field to a double stile over a stream and ahead again to a stile out on to a road.

Turn left up the road past the entrance to Brockham Park and up the hill. The buses stop on this road. Opposite a cricket ground take the track on the right and cross the field to the corner, where the path narrows through a copse and emerges at a bridleway post. Cross the track to a grassy path and, ignoring side turnings, continue ahead to a T junction. Turn left on a wide grassy ride, passing bridleway signs, and in the clearing take the narrow path slightly right ahead through the posts to re-enter the pinewoods and so retrace one's steps to the car park.

16. Chessington, Epsom Common and Ashtead Common

Distance: 7½ or 5½ miles.
Grid reference: 179634.
Ordnance Survey maps: 1:50,000 sheet 187; 1:25,000 sheets TQ06/16, TQ15.

This walk takes you across farm land and the Horton Country Park to the large pond in Epsom Common. The longer walk extends across to Ashtead Common and both return via the outskirts of Chessington Zoo and Winey Hill. This is not a suitable walk for wet weather as some of the paths on the commons may become waterlogged.

Trains: Chessington South station.

Bus: Number 65 stops outside the station.
Car park: There is a car park at Chessington South station.

From the station turn left and after about 50 yards turn right up a footpath between some houses. Continue on this path until you reach open land with fine views across to Epsom and Ashtead commons. Turn left on a path with blackberry bushes on the left and, keeping houses on the left, continue forward to a small road by a block of flats. Cross the road to a public footpath between hedges, signposted to Epsom. This path leads down past a noisy dogs' boarding kennels, over a barred fence to a ford. Cross the ford and continue forward, over a double bar and along the edge of a field. At the top of the field turn right and after a short distance there is a stile in the trees on the left. Cross this to a small path and continue forward when this soon meets a wide track. After about a quarter of a mile, keep on past a footpath sign to the left by a white house and continue on for about another half a mile, through two six-barred gates, and, crossing a track by a house, cross the Horton Country Park to a swing gate out on to a road.

Turn right up the road, bear right at a fork by riding stables, and when the road bends right into a hospital, continue forward along a churned-up bridle track. At the end of the track cross the road slightly right to a path leading into Epsom Common. After a few yards turn right on to a bridle track and then first left down a grassy footpath passing under a bar. At an oak standing between two paths, bear right over a small wooden bridge towards the large pond or small lake. Continue along the path with the lake on the right, passing a bench. At the end of the lake the walks divide.

For the shorter walk (5½ miles)
At the end of the lake turn right and continue along the top side of the lake crossing over a track. Turn left away from the lake at a T junction, rejoining the side of the lake shortly. Near the earth barrier separating the original Stew Pond from the new lake, turn left under a bar and continue ahead over three crossing tracks, eventually reaching a horse ride enclosed by wooden railings. Cross the ride to the path opposite by a beech tree with two peculiar rings round its trunk. After a few minutes walk keep to the right fork and continue on this definite path.

For the longer walk (7½ miles)
At the bench by the end of the lake, turn left over a stile and take the path half-right which leads over a planked bridge. Continue forward and then take the first turning on the left with a copse on the right. Go over a crossing track and on to a wide grassy track. Turn right with a bar in the distance. After passing

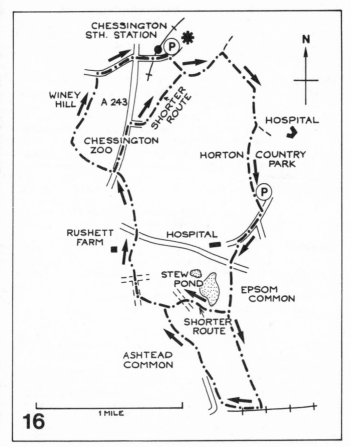

N

CHESSINGTON
STH. STATION

WINEY
HILL

A 243

SHORTER
ROUTE

HOSPITAL

CHESSINGTON
ZOO

HORTON   COUNTRY
PARK

RUSHETT
FARM

HOSPITAL

STEW
POND

EPSOM
COMMON

SHORTER
ROUTE

ASHTEAD
COMMON

1 MILE

16

the bar turn right on to a chalky path and keep on this path for some way until it emerges on to a horse ride. Turn left and continue up to the railway line. Turn right and then half-right away from the railway. Keeping in line with some pylons, continue ahead until you reach the backs of some houses, where you turn right. On reaching a path by a stream, go left over a bridge and at a fork keep right. At the next fork turn right into the trees and bear left on a path through the trees. At a crossing track turn right and keep on this track until it comes to a small T junction. Turn right into more open heathland. Ignore a small left

57

fork and at a Y fork at a clearing keep left. Keep forward when a path joins from the left. At a wide junction of paths by a beech tree with an arrow, go left of the beech on a slightly rising path through bracken and silver birch. Turn left at a crossing path and continue ahead.

For both walks

The two walks now continue together by keeping to the right of other paths and eventually reaching a main crossing track. Turn right for a short distance to a gate leading to a field. There is one of the 'iron men' posts here. These were boundary posts erected in 1851 to mark the edge of the Metropolitan Police District, where tolls on coal and wine brought into London were levied.

Cross the field diagonally right on the track, coming out on to a road by a public footpath sign. Cross to another sign opposite and follow this rather boggy path to the main road by Chessington Zoo. It is possible after some way to take a track in the woods on the left used by motorcycle scramblers. (On reaching the road by the zoo a short cut back to the station can be taken by turning right past the zoo to Chalky Lane. After passing the football club ground turn left through metal posts at a bend in the lane. After about half a mile, bear left at a stream across the path into a field and continue with a hedge on the right. Turn left up the field on a path and at the top turn right back to a footpath between houses. Turn left for the station, bus and car park.)

For the return past Chessington Zoo, cross the main road to a footpath signposted to Claygate. Follow the perimeter of the zoo up the hill to the next footpath sign, where you turn right by the spotted deer enclosure. There are fine views here across to Claygate and the new lake by the side of the Esher bypass. Chessington Zoo occupies the site of Burnt Stub, a fourteenth-century house burned down to a 'stub' by Parliamentarians during the Civil War. Continue past the zoo through a wooden enclosure on to Winey Hill. With the fence on the right cross the hill to a little lane by Barwell Court. Turn right and continue on to the main road. Cross to Garrison Lane opposite and on to Chessington South station.

17. Reigate Hill, Gatton Park and Merstham

Distance: 6 or 7 miles.
Grid reference: 263523.
Ordnance Survey maps: 1:50,000 sheet 187; 1:25,000 sheet TQ25.

This walk follows the North Downs Way to the east from Reigate

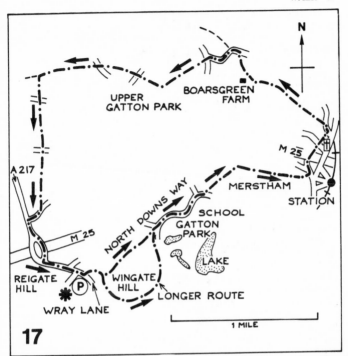

Hill, through Gatton Park, to Merstham and returns on the other side of the motorway through fields and lanes.

Trains: From the station at Merstham turn left up Station Road to the main road. Turn right to the corner by the Feathers and take the road ahead marked 'No through road'. Continue the walk at the paragraph marked (*).

Buses: The 405, 414, 440 and 455 buses stop in Merstham. Follow the directions from the Feathers as above. Alternatively, the 406 and 422 buses to Redhill stop after the large roundabout on the A217 just before Reigate Hill. Cross Gatton Bottom Lane to the National Trust and North Downs Way signs on the left of Wray Lane opposite the car park.

Car park: After the large roundabout on the A217 over the M25, fork left then immediately right to the car park in Wray Lane at the top of Reigate Hill.

Refreshments: In the car park on Reigate Hill or in Merstham.

From the car park cross Wray Lane at the entrance of the car park to the North Downs Way signpost and follow the path to the right down the hill. A very pleasant extra mile's walking can be taken at this point through the wood to a fine viewpoint looking over Gatton Lake and the Surrey Weald.

For the longer walk, when the path bends to the left continue forward down to a wood. After passing some wooden rails bear off left round a dip and continue along this path until it forks at a single beech tree. Keep right through this beautiful wood, which is a mass of bluebells in season. At a T junction turn left along a wide track down the hill. The view here across to the large lake at Gatton Park and beyond over Surrey to the Sussex Weald is breathtaking. At the bottom of the hill turn left, soon passing a smaller lake on the right. Continue to the top of the rise to join the North Downs Way by turning right through Gatton Park.

The shorter walk continues on the main path to the bottom of the hill and at the cottage at the bottom turn right down a metalled lane passing the Royal Alexandra and Albert School and Hospital in Gatton Park. (Gatton Hall was once owned by the Colman family of mustard fame.)

Both walks now follow the North Downs Way signs through the park and at the North Lodge go through the gates. Still following the North Downs Way signs, bear to the left at the Orpington Nurseries and keep forward past a drive leading to the house. At the end of the nurseries by an old gate take the footpath on the left between fences, climb the stile into some fields and follow the path over stiles, past Merstham cricket ground into Merstham itself.

(*)Turn left along the aptly named Quality Street, which was once part of the old road to Croydon until the present road was built in 1807. It is said to owe its present name to a reference to Barrie's play of the same name in which Sir Seymour Hicks and his wife, Ellaline Terriss, were acting. They lived in the Old Forge House, which is marked as a building of special interest at the end of the street on the right. Turn down the passage beside it, crossing the motorway by the footbridge to the lane ahead.

We now leave the North Downs Way by crossing this lane to some stone steps opposite. Go through the wooden gate and turn sharp left up some steps, skirting the church on the right. Follow the path to some steps up on to a lane. Turn left and just before a white house on the left, about 150 yards, turn left on to a footpath. In November hundreds of pheasants could be seen in the fields and woods here. After a while cross two stiles close together and then go diagonally left across a field to a farm and barn in the hollow. Cross a stile at the left end of the hedge and bear up the hill towards some feeding cages at the top of the field. Continue along the farm track to a footpath sign and stile on the right just before a farmyard. Keep to the left-hand fence, crossing a barrier on to a farm track. Turn right down the lane to a minor road. A fine house can be seen in the distance on the right.

Turn left down the lane for about a quarter of a mile to a T junction. Turn left again for about 25 yards to a stile in the hedge on the right. Cross the stile and walk up the left-hand side of the field to a stile in the corner. Continue in the same direction with a coppice now on the right to cross a stile at the next corner. On entering a wood keep on in the same direction – bluebells are abundant here – past a pillbox and over another stile. Continue forward with views of Upper Gatton Park on the left, over a further stile and finally out to a lane by a cottage.

Cross the road to a stile in the hedge and keep on in the same direction, passing a clump of trees on the right. Keep the wire fence on the right and at the end of the field cross the stile to another stile over the road, to the left of a cottage with a very pretty garden. Follow the path over another stile, eventually coming out on to a farm lane. Turn left and continue forward towards the farm. Turn right past the gate up the track (if very muddy here, keep up the field on the right before the gate). At the top of the field turn left by a footpath sign to Reigate Hill. Continue past some fine houses out on to a road. Cross this to a kissing gate opposite and cross the field with the hedge on the left. Go through another kissing gate and continue in the same direction towards a small but beautifully kept mobile homes park. Cross the stile to take the path running alongside the caravans out to a road. Cross Blackhorse Lane and walk along the main A217 road towards the roundabout. Cross the M25 slip road and walk across the bridge over the M25. Turn left up the main Reigate road past the bus stop and cross Gatton Bottom Lane to Wray Lane with the car park on the right.

18. Caterham, Arthur's Seat and Paddock Barn

Distance: 7 miles.
Grid reference: 337554.
Ordnance Survey maps: 1:50,000 sheet 187; 1:25,000 sheet TQ35.

A lovely walk from Caterham following the North Downs Way over White Hill and Gravelly Hill with superb views to the south on a clear day, returning to Caterham via field paths.

Trains: Caterham station. From the station entrance turn right up Church Hill to St Mary's church on the right at the top. The footpath entrance is by a bus stop on the left just past the church.
Buses: 409, 411, 440 buses stop just past St Mary's church,

or 197 in Caterham. Follow the directions from the station.
Car park: There is a small car park by St Mary's church on the B2030, Caterham, or free parking at Caterham station at weekends or in a car park just off the roundabout in Caterham.
Refreshments: In Caterham or at the inn near Arthur's Seat.

The walk starts by turning left down the footpath by the bus stop which is just past St Mary's church on the top of Church Hill, Caterham. Opposite St Mary's church is the ancient downland church of St Lawrence, which is still used for some services. The path is enclosed by laurel hedges and railings at first but soon emerges at a large recreation park (toilets here on the right by the tennis courts). Keep on the path ahead, which runs alongside the back gardens of some houses, and at the end of the park continue through a wooden barrier in the same direction past a small cul-de-sac and on another enclosed path with first a nursery garden and then a fine open space on the left. Go down through another barrier and cross the road to a pleasant residential avenue opposite going gently uphill. At the end of this avenue turn left and then right down Birchwood Lane. This lane soon leaves houses behind to continue with fields on either side. When it peters out in some woods turn left at a signpost for the Pilgrims' Way. Keep on this path with a fence on the left until you come to a stile ahead into a field. Cross the field with the fence on the right and over another stile on to the Pilgrims' Way.

Turn left along the Pilgrims' Way and at a farm turn right on a footpath leading past the farm and an old barn on to a metalled track between fields. Climb over a stepped metal fence to continue on a cart track. Where the path goes steeply downhill at the corner of the field, keep left between a field and a hedge, then bear right through brick gateposts out on to a road.

Cross to the road opposite, soon passing a folly tower on the left called Arthur's Seat. Continue along the North Downs Way, which follows this road for about three quarters of a mile to some crossroads, and take the North Downs Way footpath, which is half-right and starts behind the Hextalls Lane sign. Keep on this path for some way, eventually passing through some green posts, and follow the acorn signs out on to a road past the viewpoint at Gravelly Hill. Turn right by the North Downs Way sign into some beautiful woods and continue to follow the acorns and blue signs for about half a mile until the path comes out on to a small road with a caravan encampment opposite.

Turn right down the road and take the path on the right parallel to the road to cross the dual carriageway in the valley by the footbridge. Cross the stile ahead to a further stile and turn right, still on the North Downs Way. After about 100 yards bear left by a stile and follow the path out to a road. Cross this to a path almost opposite and when this path emerges at a track with a

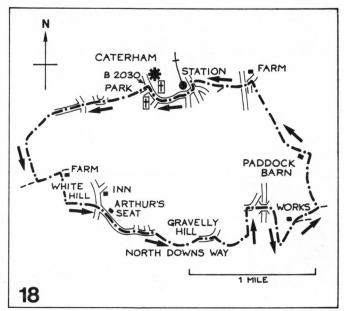

N

CATERHAM

B 2030
PARK

STATION

FARM

FARM
WHITE
HILL

INN
ARTHUR'S
SEAT

PADDOCK
BARN

WORKS

GRAVELLY
HILL

NORTH DOWNS WAY

1 MILE

18

house on the right leave the North Downs Way to take the path ahead steeply uphill through the woods with a large works on the left. Continue uphill to cross a wire fence with wooden slats and a yellow waymark and bear left following a small path to a huge beech tree with a broken wooden stile on the left. Go over this into a field and keep forward uphill with a wire fence on the left. At the corner of the field cross the stile and keep a fence to a field on the right to pass some farm buildings. Turn left at the end of the farm and follow the track past a corrugated iron fence on the left. At the end of the fence turn right and continue on this cart track for about a mile on a wide ridge with good views to left and right (in winter). On reaching some buildings, turn left and left again down a drive.

When the drive nears the dual carriageway, go over some mounds on the right by a cart track and down some steps to cross through the barrier of the busy main road to a stone footpath sign opposite. Follow the path down towards Caterham and, where it forks, keep right alongside a wire fence. When the path emerges on to a road, keep forward into Caterham. Turn left to the roundabout and then right past the station. Keep up Church Hill for the car park.

Index